Professional Development as Transformative Learning

Professional Development as Transformative Learning

New Perspectives for Teachers of Adults

Patricia Cranton

Jossey-Bass Publishers • San Francisco

Substantial discounts on bulk quantities of Jossey-Bass books are available to corporations, professional associations, and other organizations. For details and discount information, contact the special sales department at Jossey-Bass Inc., Publishers (415) 433–1740; Fax (800) 605–2665.

For sales outside the United States, please contact your local Simon & Schuster International office.

TCF Manufactured in the United States of America on Lyons Falls Pathfinder Tradebook. This paper is acid-free and 100 percent totally chlorine-free.

Library of Congress Cataloging-in-Publication Data

Cranton, Patricia.
Professional development as transformative learning: New perspectives for teachers of adults / Patricia Cranton.
     p.   cm.—(The Jossey-Bass higher and adult education series)
  Includes bibliographical references and index.
  ISBN 0-7879-0197-0
  1. Adult education teachers—Training of.   2. Adult education teachers—In-service training. 3. Critical thinking. 4. Adult learning. I. Title. II. Series.
LC5225.T4.C73   1996
370'.71'2—dc20   95-36272
                                               CIP

FIRST EDITION
HB Printing   10 9 8 7 6 5 4 3 2 1

**The Jossey-Bass
Higher and Adult Education Series**

Consulting Editor
Adult and Continuing Education

Alan B. Knox
University of Wisconsin, Madison

Contents

Preface

Adult educators come from backgrounds as diverse as the settings in which they practice. Their preparation for the role of educator is often minimal. Expertise in a subject area may be considered by organizations and by educators themselves to be the primary prerequisite of becoming an adult educator. Our growth and development tend to come from experience and trial-and-error practice. It is my intent in this book to draw on recent adult education theoretical work, especially transformative learning theory, and use it to understand how we learn about our practice.

Background

In the adult education literature, we have moved toward theory building in which the complexity of self-directed learning is recognized, critical reflection is emphasized, and transformative learning is seen to be a goal. Stephen Brookfield led this shift in thinking in 1986 with his book *Understanding and Facilitating Adult Learning*. He challenged the notion that educators assume the role of "automatons" meeting the expressed needs of self-directed adults, a notion that then had had a stranglehold on practice, theory, and research for decades. In 1987, Brookfield further contributed to the field with his *Developing Critical Thinkers,* a practical guide to stimulating alternative ways of thinking and learning. Candy (1991) increased our understanding of self-directed learning with his comprehensive analysis and integration of philosophical, theoretical, and research-based views of the concept.

Although Jack Mezirow's work on transformative learning had actually begun in the late 1970s, his work tended to remain an interesting footnote in the literature until this shift in thinking took place. Following his comprehensive theoretical description *Transformative Dimensions of Adult Learning* in 1991, the interest of researchers, practitioners, and theorists has been sparked. What we need now is to see how these challenging theoretical concepts help us as educators learn about our own practice.

Need

Most professionals receive training and education in their field. There are always questions as to the quality and content of preparatory programs; nevertheless people do have the opportunity to learn about their profession. Following the initial training, most professionals are then encouraged to participate in professional development activities of one kind or another. In some professions, continuing education is voluntary; in others it is a requirement of maintaining certification.

For most adult educators, none of this is so. They often need not have preparatory training, and professional development offerings may not be available or appropriate. How do adult educators learn about their practice? How do they continue to grow and change over time? How can they go beyond the acquisition of simple techniques to a deeper reflection on and understanding of their work? We regularly ask these questions about adult learning, and we dedicate considerable thought, research, and writing to addressing them. What we also need to do is apply this expertise to understanding our *own* development.

Purpose and Audience

In this book I intend

- To review the nature of adult educator practice and the traditional professional development strategies
- To apply our current knowledge about self-directed learning, critical reflection, and transformative learning to understanding our development as educators
- To suggest practical strategies for educator development that are self-directed, reflective, and transformative
- To describe educator development in work and social contexts and to propose a model of the influences on our development

My primary audience is practicing adult educators who are interested in developing a deeper understanding of their work. Practitioners are provided with a challenging and provocative way of thinking about their own growth and development as educators. They are stimulated to engage in critical reflection on their practice and to articulate their perspectives on their work.

Another audience is university faculty and graduate students in departments of adult, higher, and continuing education. This book seeks to lead students to develop their approaches to practice; they will also be interested in the implications for research. The book can serve as a supplementary textbook for graduate-level courses. It is of interest to scholars, writers, and researchers in adult education.

Finally, instructional developers in higher education; human resource personnel in government, business, and industry; and professional developers in the health professions will find the book useful for their practice.

Overview of the Contents

I first review the current state of professional development practices. I then bring in theoretical conceptualizations of adult learning in order to build a model of and a practical approach to adult educator development. Although the field of adult education is now mature enough to support several philosophies or traditions, I primarily follow the thinking of Brookfield and Mezirow.

Chapter One provides an overview of the diverse contexts within which educators work and the nature of professional development in those contexts. I discuss the different kinds of human interests and knowledge that are relevant to educator practice.

In Chapter Two, I elaborate on specific strategies that are traditionally used in professional development, considering each in terms of the type of knowledge it fosters and its congruence with educators' practice.

The book then shifts to the three central concepts in adult education theory: self-directed learning, critical reflection, and transformative learning.

In Chapter Three, I describe educators' development in terms of Candy's (1991) four facets of self-direction (personal autonomy, self-management, learner control, and autodidaxy). Critical reflection is the theme for Chapter Four. Using Brookfield's (1987) components of critical thinking as a basis, since they are parallel to the processes of transformative learning, I discuss how educators' development can be critical in nature. Similarly, in Chapter Five, Mezirow's (1991) theory of transformation is applied to the development of our practice.

Although we pay considerable attention to individual differences among learners, we rarely talk about the influence of educators' characteristics on their work. I use Jung's ([1921] 1971) psychological type theory to do this in Chapter Six. But individual differences are just one aspect of development. In Chapter Seven, I discuss working toward change in organizations and institutions, within the community of educators, and in our society.

The central processes of self-direction, critical reflection, and transformative learning are influenced by educators' individual differences. These processes also take place within a teaching context that is a part of an organization or community in a culture. In Chapter Eight, I present a model depicting the influences on educators' development and, in turn, educators' influences on their context and culture.

Who are the developers who work with educators to foster change? How can they ensure that their practice encourages self-directed, reflective, and transformative development? Chapter Nine addresses these questions with the presentation of strategies for developers.

Acknowledgments

I would like to acknowledge the learners and colleagues with whom I have worked to develop my educational practice. Among them, Carolin Kreber remains my best critic and strongest supporter.

The thinking and writing of Jack Mezirow and Stephen Brookfield continually deepen my understanding of adult education theory.

I am grateful for all of the assistance I have received from Jossey-Bass—the comments and encouragement of Alan Knox, the suggestions of the anonymous reviewers, and the practical advice and support from Gale Erlandson and Rachel Livsey.

Most of all, I want to thank Robert Knoop for his intuitive understanding of my work.

St. Catharines, Ontario   PATRICIA CRANTON
December 1995

The Author

PATRICIA CRANTON is professor of education at Brock University. She received her B.Ed. degree (1971) from the University of Calgary in English literature and mathematics, her M.Sc. degree (1973), also from the University of Calgary, in computer applications, and her Ph.D. degree from the University of Toronto in measurement, evaluation, and computer applications.

Cranton's main research interests have been the evaluation of teaching in higher education, instructional development, self-directed learning, and transformative learning. She was selected as a Distinguished Scholar at Brock University in 1991 in recognition of her research and writing. She received the Ontario Confederation of University Faculty Association's Teaching Award in 1993 and the Lieutenant Governor's Laurel Award in 1994 for an outstanding contribution to university teaching. Cranton's books include *Planning Instruction for Adult Learners* (1989), *Working with Adult Learners* (1992), and *Understanding and Promoting Transformative Learning: A Guide for Educators of Adults* (1994).

Cranton was at McGill University from 1976 to 1986 in the Centre for Teaching and Learning and the Department of Educational Psychology and Counselling.

Professional Development as Transformative Learning

Preparation and Development of Adult Educators

Educators are learners. In this book, I describe educators' growth and development as a process of becoming more autonomous and independent, of engaging in critical reflection, and of revising perspectives on practice.

Whether we do it informally or formally, systematically or haphazardly, as practicing adult educators we are learning about teaching. The human resource developer planning another workshop, the nutritionist leading another seminar, or the counselor meeting another client thinks about what he or she is doing. When something works, we note that and decide to try that approach again; when something does not go quite right, we wonder what we could do differently next time. Often, we get feedback from our learners, either through a structured questionnaire or from anecdotal comments, and that information leads us to learn about our practice. Sometimes, as educators, we choose to attend a workshop on an innovative method, or we even enroll in degree or certificate programs in education. Also, our organization may require participation in some professional development activities. On many levels and in different ways, educators learn about their practice.

In this chapter, I describe how an educator's development can be transformative and illustrate this with a case. I review the variety of contexts within which adult educators practice, and I discuss how educators in these contexts learn about their teaching. Finally,

I use Habermas's (1971) framework of human interests as a way of thinking about educators' perspectives on their work.

Transformative Learning About Our Practice

Transformative learning occurs when an individual has reflected on assumptions or expectations about what will occur, has found these assumptions to be faulty, and has revised them (Cranton, 1994a; Mezirow, 1991). When reflection focuses on premises (that is, why is this important in the first place?), it has the potential to lead to transformed meaning perspectives or changed ways of seeing the world. This is the process of emancipatory learning—becoming free from forces that have limited our options, forces that have been taken for granted or seen as beyond our control.

How do we learn about teaching? As I discuss in this chapter, most adult educators learn about teaching through their experiences. The learning may focus on techniques: how to prepare a good agenda, how to manage the time in a session, how to speak clearly. Learning about teaching involves understanding other people: the differences among individuals, how people get along with each other, the expectations and values of the learners and the community. Becoming a better teacher also includes questioning and thinking critically about one's own practice.

It is generally agreed in the literature (Brookfield, 1987; Boud and Walker, 1991; Tennant and Pogson, 1995) that critical reflection is the key to learning from experience. Educators learn about teaching by talking about their experiences, becoming aware of the assumptions and expectations they have, questioning these assumptions, and possibly revising their perspectives. It is this process that forms the basis for my discussion of educators' development in this book.

A Case Illustration

The experience of an instructional development client of mine may help to illustrate the process of critical reflection as a way of learning about teaching. This description is used with permission from the client, but his name and discipline have been changed to preserve his anonymity.

Tim, a senior science professor, came to my office about three years ago and asked me to help him develop an evaluation form to give to his students at the end of a course. His department chair had requested that faculty administer such a form. Tim had taught in the sciences for almost thirty years; he had always regarded himself as a competent teacher and was slightly annoyed that he was required to demonstrate his competence to anyone. After a discussion of Tim's approach to teaching, we developed an appropriate form.

That year, he administered the form. Some time later he brought the results to me for discussion. Students rated him highly, though there was an indication that he intimidated some students who were not science majors. We discussed this, but Tim was not overly concerned.

The following year, Tim administered the same form and again brought the results to me. Students' reactions of being overwhelmed by the content, intimidated by Tim's style, and anxious about the pace of the course were even stronger, although they gave high ratings on other aspects of the course.

At the beginning of the next year, Tim initiated a project to more thoroughly investigate his teaching. He was near retirement now and wanted to understand his practice before leaving it. He thought that there might be "some small things he could do to improve in his last year." We made plans to videotape several of his classes, collect feedback from students for the videotaped sessions, and view and discuss the videotapes. Tim gave me copies of his class notes and kept a log of his thoughts on his practice. I invited a graduate student assistant to join us, to give another perspective and form a team for the project.

As we entered the process, Tim did not appear to take it too seriously. He made jokes about his own style and frequently commented that it was rather silly to take up so much of my time since he was retiring soon. The first two videotapes clearly reflected what the students had been describing as an intimidating style. The pace was frantic; students were called upon by name to respond to questions to which they did not know the answer. We continually stopped the videotape and asked Tim, "What are you doing here?" "Do you see that student's reaction to your question?" "Why did you push on to the next topic at this point?"

The third videotape was notably different. Tim spoke in a softer voice. He seemed more relaxed. He did not once call on a student by name to respond to a question. When we commented on this change, Tim strongly denied having made any changes at all. He explained that the topic was different in this session and, therefore, maybe the tape looked different.

After the Christmas break, the next videotape showed some return to the original style but was still softer and more relaxed than in the first two tapes. The feedback from students had not changed in nature. However, at the beginning of the process, there had been observable anxiety: students had left the room and later explained to us that they were too frightened of being called on to stay in the room. This behavior had stopped.

It was near the end of the academic year, eight months into the project, when Tim, very directly and openly, described to us what the process meant to him. He had been led, he said, to question not only his current practice but his practice over the past thirty years. He had always seen his practice in one way; now he saw it in another way. He described this as a difficult and painful, but also enlightening and amazing, experience. I expressed concern: who wants to come to that kind of conclusion about thirty years of practice? But Tim was delighted. He made arrangements to teach "one more course" after his retirement, and he planned to show one of the videotapes to his next class as a way of stimulating discussion about his teaching. He expressed interest in writing an article about his experience, and he mailed me some of his notes on what the article might contain.

Tim's development was transformative learning. While I was concerned about the devastating effect that such an experience might have, Tim used the words "I feel freed somehow" to describe it. Emancipatory learning can be described as freedom from "forces that limit our options and our rational control over our lives but have been taken for granted or seen as beyond human control" (Mezirow, 1991, p. 87). Tim did not simply learn how to use the overhead projector more efficiently; he changed his entire view of his practice.

Educator development of this nature is self-directed. The individual chooses to examine his or her practice and retains control over the process. Self-directed development is discussed in Chapter Three. It involves critical self-reflection: an articulation of assumptions about practice and a questioning of those assumptions (elaborated in Chapter Four). When assumptions are found to be invalid or constraining and when those assumptions are revised, as were Tim's assumptions, transformative learning takes place. I describe this process in more detail in Chapter Five.

Adult Educators: Who Are We?

I chose Tim's case from the university context because that is one setting in which I work, but Tim could as easily have been a manager in a government department or a trainer in industry.

Educators work in content areas and with specific groups of learners. We are learners of our discipline and students of our clientele. We keep up to date by attending conferences, reading journals, and perhaps formally studying our discipline. This learning, too, feeds into our practice.

Adult educator roles, the settings within which adult educators work, and the nature of adult educators' preparation for their practice are diverse. To name but a few examples, distinctive fields of practice include health education, continuing professional education, adult basic education, community action, management training, parent education, faculty development, literacy training, and religious education. The American Association for Adult and Continuing Education offers members a choice of thirty-five units with which they may affiliate. These units are grouped into seven categories primarily based on types of programs (for example, life skills, military), learner groups (elderly, business and industry), or services (colleges, libraries). Similarly, examples of adult educator role descriptions are instructor, facilitator, resource person, manager, change agent, or co-learner. The roles are sometimes classified into groups, put onto continua, or seen as adversarial positions reflecting different philosophies of practice.

No one theory of adult learning informs all educators. No one model describes educator practice. No one paradigm underlies adult education research. No one philosophical perspective determines the goals and responsibilities of adult education. Most educators identify themselves with their subject area, their clientele, the type of organization within which they work, or even the medium they employ (such as computer technology) rather than with adult education as a profession or discipline. This lack of a common identity hinders the development of the discipline, but it especially interferes with our conception of how adult educators are prepared and how they continue to develop as professionals. There are limited conferences, courses, and written materials that practicing educators actually access. If content expertise or familiarity with a certain learner group, organization, or medium is seen to be the primary prerequisite for practicing as an adult educator, educator development becomes a splintered array of activities designed to increase knowledge and understanding in disconnected fields.

What we do not often do is examine our commonalities as educators, and especially our commonalities as learners in the discipline of adult education. If you are a trainer on safety regulations for workers in industry, or a nurse educator, or a college instructor in the English department, and I am a teacher of adult educators, we share the common goal of wanting to foster learning in others. We also share the common goal of wanting to be better practitioners.

A strong theoretical and practical literature is now beginning to emerge in adult education. True, it is not informed by one perspective, but perhaps that is not an ideal state given the kaleidoscope of activities included under the adult education umbrella. We are, though, witnessing a stage of development in the field that is reflective, critical, and fairly comprehensive. That is, we are beginning to understand how adults learn and how educators can foster, support, and challenge that learning. What we seem not to have realized is that the literature applies equally to us as we learn about teaching. What we know about how our learners engage in self-directed learning, critical reflection, transformative learning, and social change will be applied to how we grow and develop as educators. We, too, are adult learners.

Educators in Context

Brookfield (1986) provides a comprehensive survey of formal and informal adult education settings. I intend here to look at and think about some common contexts with a view to considering educator development strategies across these contexts. The contexts chosen are universities, colleges, business and industry, health professions, community education, and informal settings (for example, community action, informal learning groups, and learning networks).

In Universities

Educators in universities are experts in their content areas. Rarely do they have formal preparation as educators, unless they are in faculties of education or working in programs such as Teaching English as a Second Language. Some university faculty have experience as teaching assistants from their days as graduate students; many do not. Even these experiences tend to be focused on selected aspects of the educator role, such as marking papers or leading seminars under the supervision of a faculty member. In other words, preparation for the educator role is minimal. Yet being an educator is a major responsibility of the position. As Rice and Richlin (1993) suggest, a scholarship of teaching and learning is even difficult to discuss. For faculty, scholarship and teaching are often seen as competing for time and attention. When asked what would facilitate their development as educators, most faculty respond that they need more time to develop their content expertise.

University faculty do not tend to describe themselves as adult educators. Because traditional university students are full-time and young adults, most faculty respond to questions related to adult education by noting that they do not have very many "adults" (mature students) in their classes. This perception is, perhaps, an explanation for the lack of intersection between the adult and higher education literatures. When Wilcox (1990) surveyed university faculty on the extent to which they saw themselves as encouraging self-directed learning, only 13 percent indicated that this was a component of their philosophy of practice. Observation of and interviews with a subgroup of this 13 percent further revealed that many of these faculty did not in fact use strategies that would actually foster self-directed learning. University educators simply do not see themselves as adult educators. They often do not even see the educator role as their primary responsibility;

rather, they see the university as an institution for the advancement of knowledge and hence see their role as one in which research in the discipline is the priority. The reward system of the university usually supports this perspective by basing promotion more on research productivity than on teaching effectiveness, in practice if not in theory.

In-service professional development in the universities is usually voluntary. Traditionally, developmental activities have consisted of short workshops on specific teaching techniques, newsletters, or grants for implementing innovative methods. Only recently has professional development in higher education turned to longer-term interactions with educators as a means of educator development (Amundsen, Gryspeerdt, and Moxness, 1993; Zuber-Skerritt, 1992).

In Colleges

The terms *colleges* and *universities* are not used in the same way across countries. By college, I refer to institutions in which teaching and service are the primary responsibilities of faculty. Nevertheless, most educators in colleges are not prepared teachers, but rather experts in a content area. There appears to be a difference, though, in the way that college educators view teaching, given that the advancement of knowledge is not a part of the mandate of the institution, and that research is not normally a component of the faculty role. Advanced degrees, or even undergraduate degrees in education, are valued and rewarded in most college systems. College faculty tend to be unionized, and the unions have tended to fight for salary scales that incorporate further education. At the university, faculty generally begin their careers with a doctorate in their discipline; at the college, this is far less likely. Advances in salary can then be linked to further studies, including educational studies.

College faculty also are unlikely to view themselves as adult educators. They see their students as young and pre-adult, or even adolescent. The demographics of college students are changing rapidly, but faculty tend to see themselves as teaching young people, not adults, with the exceptions of upgrading programs, retraining programs, and some special programs for mature students.

Some colleges mandate professional development in education or even certification in adult education (for example, the New

Brunswick community college system in Canada), but these are exceptions. Colleges in Ontario have as mandatory thirty days annually of professional development for all faculty, but they do not specify what that development should entail. As in the university systems, educator development tends to be an offering of short-term workshops and seminars. It is more likely that college faculty participate in instructional development, as they are more likely to see teaching as a crucial part of their role.

In Business and Industry

In business and industry, we often find individuals who think of themselves as trainers rather than educators, although the literature increasingly emphasizes teamwork, and leaders and managers are described as people developers (for example, see Watkins and Marsick, 1993). Individuals in the positions of human resource developer, trainer, or training manger tend to have degrees in business administration, organizational behavior, or management. Rarely does their educational background include adult education. Trainers tend to follow a model leading to instrumental knowledge in their work; educational technology with an emphasis on needs assessment, learning objectives, task analysis, and performance evaluation dominates the field. This is so even when an organization describes itself as "moving from training to a learning environment," as did Exxon Research and Engineering in a case study presented by Watkins and Marsick (1993, pp. 49–52). At Exxon, Employee Development Planning Maps are arranged as grids where the employee can list the "specific knowledge and skills to be learned in the coming year" (p. 51).

Traditionally, training has been based on the assumption that the causes of problems are knowledge and skill deficits. Trainers address these problems by delivering programs in which the trainees are the recipients. However, there has been little agreement among employers as to what training should be or what value it may have. For example, in one survey, Keenan (1990) found that one-half of the respondents felt their sales would not be affected if training programs for salespeople were eliminated.

Changes in the nature of the workplace, the nature of work, and the structure of organizations are now leading to a shift in focus in the world of training. A skill learned this week may be out of date next week when the new equipment arrives. There is a call for generic skills such as problem solving and critical thinking. Organizational changes such as the "flattening" of the traditional hierarchical management structure have led to new roles for managers. Teamwork, participative decision making, staff empowerment, and effective delegation are some of the new key words for managers.

Seen to be representative of such a shift in focus is Rosenberg's (1990) description of the four areas of *human performance technology*, an umbrella term for training programs: human resource development (the improvement of individuals); organizational development (the improvement of groups and systems); human resource management (the management of the performance of individuals); and environmental engineering (the provision of tools and facilities to support improved performance). The language still rings of technical interests, even in the use of the word *technology*, but it is described as a set of values, principles, and strategies. Along the same lines, it is interesting to note that the American Society for Training and Development lists "adult learning understanding" as a "technical competency" required of trainers (McLagan, 1989).

How trainers are prepared for their roles and how they engage in professional development varies widely. In North America, there are no consistent policies for becoming a trainer or procedures for receiving accreditation as a trainer, though there are programs designed for this purpose. One such example is the Training and Human Resource Development Certificate Program at Florida International University (Castner and Jordan, 1989). It is interesting that Adult Education Theory is included as one of the five core courses in the curriculum of this program. Wilson (1992) reports on training and professional development approaches in Australia, Germany, Japan, and Great Britain, among others. It is the German training infrastructure that includes the most developed train-the-trainers component. For example, 560 training programs for trainers, each including 120 hours, were offered in Berlin alone in one year. Unfortunately, it seems that the available literature does not address the nature of these programs.

On a more informal level, educators in business and industry choose to attend workshops, read journals such as *Training and*

Development, and belong to professional associations such as the National Society for Performance and Instruction and the American Society for Training and Development. McLagan (1987) emphasizes the importance of networking and individual planning of professional development activities. Watkins and Marsick (1993) emphasize that learning can be "intentionally planned, serendipitously discovered, incidentally absorbed, or retrospectively revealed" (p. 47). Similarly, Baskett (1993) argues that continuing professional educators need to reframe their understanding of their roles to include "non-educational solutions" such as promoting peer and team learning, reconfiguring the workplace structure so as to be more conducive to informal learning, helping professionals learn from life transformation, and enabling reflection on learning and practice.

In a needs analysis, Geis (1991) concludes that the role of continuing professional development "in the field of training has never been more critical than it is now" (p. 3). Yet activities in this area remain relatively isolated from the potential contributions of adult education theory and practice and seem to retain their emphasis on technical knowledge despite some rhetoric to the contrary.

In the Health Professions

Educators in the health professions primarily associate themselves with their profession rather than with education. In this way, they are similar to university and college faculty; indeed, those educators who are involved in the preparatory training of health professionals often work within an institution of higher education. They usually have a background of professional practice which precedes their entry into educator roles.

Adult educators working in the health professions are found in a wide variety of roles: training would-be professionals in medicine, nursing, dentistry, or dental hygiene in a college or university; conducting continuing education programs and workshops for practicing professionals; acting in staff development roles for hospitals or other institutions much in the same way as does a trainer employed by an organization; working with patients or clients to increase their ability to manage their own health care; working with professional associations to design curriculum, develop professional standards, and evaluate future practitioners for certification; and, designing or conducting educational programs for clients, patients, or the public in general, such as smoking cessation programs, prenatal classes, or nutritional information sessions.

In the health professions, educators tend to be trained only in their profession, although their presence in graduate education programs is noticeable. At the Ontario Institute for Studies in Education, for example, the presence of health professionals in the Higher Education Group was so strong that the department designed a specialization for graduate students in that area. Professional development for practitioners, as for adult educators in other contexts, tends to consist of voluntary attendance at workshops and seminars, independent learning through reading, and participation in professional associations and conferences. However, there is something different about adult educators in the health professions. In addition to their involvement in formal degree programs in education, they support an unusually large number of journals related to educational issues (for example, *Journal of Nursing Education, Journal of Continuing Education in the Health Professions, Teaching and Learning in Medicine, Medical Education, Journal of Dental Education*), and they seem to be especially interested in their development as educators. In my ten years of instructional development experience at a large university with faculties of medicine, nursing, dentistry, and physical and occupational therapy, I noted that the health professionals stood out in their participation rate in workshops and consultations.

Another interesting aspect of educators' development in the health professions is the discrepancy between their subject area and their educator role in terms of the nature of the relevant knowledge. Most of the discipline's knowledge is based on a medical model; that is, it is technical knowledge derived through empirical-analytical methodologies. This is changing to some extent in professions such as nursing and occupational therapy, but even so, the change is reluctant and gradual among practitioners. Health professionals as educators are dealing with both technical knowledge (seeing themselves as imparting that knowledge to others) and practical or communicative knowledge. They may have difficulties with the different perspectives and treat the technical knowledge as all-pervasive, imposing it onto interactions with learners and patients. This tendency is apparent, for example, in the emphasis on Bandura's (1977) social learning theory as a framework for discussing "patient compliance" in the nursing education literature. Similarly, Crowe-Joong (1993) points out the isolation of the problem-based learning curriculum in medical education from the more communicative knowledge base of the adult education literature. Curry, Wergin, and their associates (1993) emphasize the changing characteristics of the professions in general, arguing that those professions based on scientific and technical knowledge will be forced to change in order to deal with the tremendous increases in that kind of knowledge.

In Community Education

Community education is used here to refer to the mixed bag of courses offered in the evening by schools, churches, the YMCA or YWCA, and colleges or universities. They are often noncredit but are sometimes for credit toward a certificate, diploma, or degree when offered by an educational institution.

This area is also referred to as *continuing education* by some institutions, and sometimes in the literature. However, continuing education is a general term, sometimes used so as to be synonymous with adult education or lifelong learning. Selman and Dampier (1991) provide several examples of the use of the term in this way. Knox (1993) writes about "adult and continuing education" as including a wide range of programs in distance education, staff development, professional education, and health education. For this reason, I use the term community education here—differentiating it from the broader conceptualization of continuing education.

Educators working in community education form an unusual group. Their offerings range in content from general interest courses (cooking, crafts, home repair) to more technical or possibly work-related topics (computer skills, time management, stress management, second languages). The purpose has been described as being "to help maintain, expand and improve individual knowledge, skills (performance) and attitudes" (Mezirow, 1988, p. 223). Virtually anyone who decides to offer a course and obtains a high enough student enrollment for the course to be cost-effective can become an adult educator in this context. Obviously, educators in these fields possess a wide array of backgrounds, and most do not have formal preparation as educators. Similarly to the groups discussed so far, they are not likely to see themselves primarily as educators; indeed, this self-perception is even more unlikely as individuals in community education tend to be teaching part-time while working full-time in their trade or profession. They come into their positions in a variety of ways. They may, for example, feel that they have a special skill they want to offer others; they may like working with people and meet that need through teaching; they may teach to obtain extra income; or they may be accumulating experience with the hope of becoming a full-time instructor.

Development opportunities for community education instructors are minimal. Part-time educators employed by a school board, college, or university are often not informed of seminars or workshops on teaching, not because they are deliberately excluded but because they are an invisible group without an office or a mailbox. They come into an institution at night and rarely interact with their full-time peers. Community educators working through noneducational organizations will have even less chance to be involved in professional development activities or discussions, especially when they do not see themselves as educators. Development will take place as the educator increases knowledge and skill in the subject area being taught and interacts with and gets feedback from learners, assuming the educator is sensitive and open to learning from students. Generally, though, community educators are a neglected species when it comes to attention being paid to their professional development. Searching the literature for references to the category of adult educator development yields little enough generally, but virtually nothing related to community education.

In Informal Settings

Based on a series of handbooks on adult learning and several reviews of practice, Brookfield (1986) identifies a variety of informal settings for adult learning. Although it could be questioned whether some of the contexts he lists are "informal" (for example, adult basic education or correctional education in prisons), others may be: community development, voluntary organizations, community action, and informal group learning. I would add to this list such settings as self-help groups, discussion groups, civil rights movements, feminist groups, and ecology movements.

Krishnamurti (1964, p. 14) writes, "Do you know what it means to learn? When you are really learning you are learning throughout your life and there is no one special teacher to learn from. Then everything teaches you—a dead leaf, a bird in flight, a smell, a tear, the rich and the poor." Adult learning takes place in all the contexts within which people work and live. Often there is no one person we would call the educator. On the other hand, informal groups may have leaders, organizers, or rotating chairs; these individuals function as adult educators. This group is further removed from the world of formal educator preparation and development than any group discussed so far.

A large proportion of adult education occurs, and has occurred historically, in informal learning groups, learning networks, and community development or community action groups. In Canada, the Antigonish Movement (Boyle, 1953), a community development program for fishermen, farmers, and industrial workers in an economically depressed region, is but one well-known example. In the United States, the Highlander Folk School in Tennessee in the 1930s supported a strike by nonunionized coal workers (Adams, 1972), thus beginning a movement to promote social change that continues to this day. In Sweden, the enrollment in study circles includes over 60 percent of the Swedish adult population; in 1981, 310,000 collaborative circles were in operation (Borgstrom and Olofsson, 1983). Today, we are only beginning to see the potential of learning networks through electronic communications (see Pierce, Glass, Young, and Soucy, 1994). Bitnet and Internet, computer networks that link millions of people, support LISTSERV, a computer program that maintains mailing lists of individuals interested in specific discussion groups. The number of lists for discussion and exchange of information grows at a rate that is beyond documentation. Ellsworth (1993) compiled a list of scholarly discussions on adult and distance education alone containing thirty-six groups and six electronic journals; the author warns readers that the lists will change.

The facilitators, leaders, and organizers of adult education in informal settings may not view themselves as educators at all. Yet, especially in the informal contexts, as can be seen in the preceding examples, they are likely to be promoting political stances, making moral judgments, or advocating their own visions of society. Brookfield (1986, p. 165) writes: "Given the plethora of possible groups, causes, settings, and activities in which educators might involve themselves, it is crucial that they evolve a philosophical rationale comprising basic principles, purposes, and criteria to guide their efforts." Brookfield (1986, 1990a, 1993) argues throughout his writings that educators cannot and should not attempt to work independently of political or moral considerations but should make their personal philosophy explicit and be aware of how it informs their practice. It becomes important that the development of all adult educators, including those not affiliated with any educational institution, be considered and discussed in the literature. It becomes equally important that writings about professional development be accessible to all adult educators. These issues will be discussed further in Chapter Six.

Educator Interests and Knowledge

One of the most helpful underpinnings to our understanding of adult learning has been Mezirow's (1991) utilization of Habermas's (1971) types of human interests and knowledge. I use this framework as a way of furthering our understanding of how we learn to teach.

Habermas's goal in his writing has been to develop a comprehensive theory of knowledge, comprehensive enough to encompass science, morality, and art. The relevance of Habermas's work to education is clear; there were thirty-two hundred published articles in the education literature between 1972 and 1987 that referenced Habermas (Ewert, 1991). Habermas's description of our interests and ways of knowing encompasses and explains much about educators' perspectives on practice.

Habermas (1971) describes three types of interests that humans have, each defining what counts as knowledge in our society. If people are interested in, for example, understanding how machines work, then having that knowledge becomes important in that society. Although these interests and forms of knowledge exist in all spheres of human life, they will be described here primarily in relation to educator practice.

Technical Interests and Instrumental Knowledge

People have a need to control and manipulate their external environment. This interest is most clearly understood in terms of people needing to satisfy their basic requirements for food and shelter. How can we best grow vegetables? How can we build a house that will withstand the wind and keep out the cold? Most scientific interests are technical in nature. Technical interests lead us to a valuing of instrumental or cause-and-effect knowledge (if we do this, that will result). We obtain instrumental knowledge through empirical-analytical investigations, or, in other words, through the traditional scientific methodologies. We set up experiments whereby we apply various conditions of fertilizer, water, sunshine, and temperature to the growing of crops and thereby determine how best to grow those crops.

What Habermas has objected to is that our technical interests and our desire for instrumental knowledge have become a pervasive ideology. We look to explain human relationships, human learning, and even our morality in terms of instrumental knowledge. Many educators express technical interests in the world around them, including their practice; however, when talking about their work, they also recognize the unscientific nature of people working and learning together.

For decades, educators have attempted to answer the question "What technique, method, or strategy can we apply which will *cause* the most learning?" Quantitative experimental designs, parallel in methodology to those used to investigate the effect of fertilizers on crops, were set up to compare instructional methods. The random assignment of learners to experimental conditions allowed researchers to make the assumption that learners in each group were "equal" in all relevant characteristics. Individual differences among learners were treated, statistically, as error of measurement.

Understanding educator effectiveness also has been treated as instrumental knowledge. The thousands of published articles on student ratings of teaching effectiveness provide one example of this quest for instrumental knowledge (see for example, a comprehensive review of this research by Marsh, 1987). On a more general level, one can easily find evidence of technical interests throughout the literature. Boshier (1988), for example, in attempting to define a conceptual framework for analyzing the training of adult educators, writes: "Since adult education is now a broad field, the possibility of agreeing on one philosophy or set of outcomes is even more improbable than in times past. The absence of *empirical data makes it necessary to resort to philosophical or other literature*" (p. 78; emphasis added). More recently, with a shift in editorship of the *Adult Education Quarterly,* the new co-editors write: "We would like to see more data-based articles published, representing a broad spectrum of important research questions and a variety of *empirically rigorous* research methodologies" (Courtney and Dirkx, 1994, p. 63; emphasis added).

Instrumental knowledge is, of course, invaluable, but does it address our interests in human learning? Is our interest in understanding our practice a technical one? Kincheloe (1991) writes: "Positivism assumes that the personal histories of individuals and the social histories of their contexts are not germane to an appreciation of an educational setting and its significance. Such contextual information is invariably ambiguous and thus complicates the reductionism, the attempt to simplify the cause and effect relationships. . . . But the rub is that human activities like education are rarely free of ambiguity, and to miss their complexity is to miss the point" (p. 56).

Practical Interests and Practical Knowledge

People's practical interests are their desire to understand others and to be understood. This includes an interest in social action designed to best meet the needs of individuals, groups, and cultures. Language (communication with others) is used to pursue our practical interests: we talk to each other, listen to each other, write to each other, and read what others have written. The knowledge defined through our pursuit of practical interests is a knowledge of social norms, traditions, and values underlying our culture, and a mutual understanding among individuals. Habermas (1971) calls this practical knowledge and describes communicative action as the resulting behavior. Communicative action is "governed by binding consensual norms, which define reciprocal expectations about behavior and which must be understood and recognized by at least two acting subjects" (p. 92). Mezirow (1991) uses the term *communicative learning* to talk about obtaining such knowledge.

How do we obtain practical knowledge? Not through empirical study, which assumes that the objects studied are concrete, stable, and constant in their responses to various conditions. Carr and Kemmis (1986, p. 88) write: "Actions cannot be observed in the same way as natural objects. They can only be interpreted by reference to the actor's motives, intentions or purposes in performing the action. To identify these motives and intentions correctly is to grasp the 'subjective meaning' the action has to the actor." It is the hermeneutic or interpretive sciences which are used to obtain practical knowledge. The methodologies used in the interpretive research paradigm have the objective of understanding meaning rather than determining cause and effect relationships. When we are interested in practical knowledge, we use language; we communicate with others; we ask "How do you see this?" and "How do you experience this?"

It seems clear that knowledge of education is practical knowledge. Education is a social activity. It involves communication among individuals with the aims of mutual understanding, meeting the needs of individuals and groups, and social change. If we hope to understand our roles as adult educators and to grow and develop within our practice, we are interested in improving our communication with and our understanding of our learners as well as the social context within which we work. Educational goals are not so definitive as to be measured by a ruler, as we measure the height of the wheat in a field receiving fertilizer X. Similarly, the strategies by which we reach these goals are not clear-cut. Every practitioner continually makes judgments while in action (Schön, 1983, 1987); these judgments are often intuitive, perhaps not even conscious, and are based on a continuously changing set of criteria and circumstances. In order to understand this process, we need to observe what we do, critically question ourselves, and reflect on our actions within their context.

Emancipatory Interests and Emancipatory Knowledge

Habermas (1984) criticizes interpretive knowledge as being too dependent on subjective understanding. Individuals' self-knowledge and social knowledge are obviously a product of their past experience: their upbringing, relations with parents and peers, and their cultural background. Carr and Kemmis (1986, p. 95) describe the dilemma this way: "Social reality is not simply something that is structured and sustained by the interpretations of individuals—it also determines the kind of interpretations of reality that are appropriate for a particular group of individuals to possess. Social structure, as well as being the *product* of the meanings and actions of individuals, itself *produces* particular meanings, ensures their continuing existence, and thereby limits the kind of actions that it is reasonable for individuals to perform." It is not that educators simply select a perspective in the same way they choose a teaching method, but rather that basic human interests define this way of seeing the world and the perspectives then go unquestioned. It is this thinking which is the foundation of Mezirow's (1991) theory of transformative learning.

Our emancipatory interests come from our desire to grow and develop. People are interested in self-knowledge, self-awareness, and an understanding of how their past has shaped their way of being. This includes a desire to be free from self- and social distortions of knowledge. The themes of freedom and fear of freedom (Fromm, 1946) have existed throughout the history of humanity. The philosophical position underlying our emancipatory interests is called *critical theory*. Critical theorists see both the empirical and the interpretive sciences as being incomplete. They emphasize emancipation through enlightenment, and they define enlightenment as coming through a process of self-reflection that reveals distorted self-knowledge and institutional domination.

An interest in emancipation leads, through critical self-reflection, to emancipatory knowledge. Mezirow (1991, p. 87) describes this knowledge as "emancipation from libidinal, linguistic, epistemic, institutional, or environmental forces that limit our options and our rational control over our lives but have been taken for granted or seen as beyond human control. These forces include the misconceptions, ideologies, and psychological distortions in prior learning that produce or perpetuate unexamined relations of dependence." The process of gaining emancipatory knowledge is transformative learning.

Habermas (1971) sees the critical social sciences as providing the appropriate research methodologies for developing emancipatory knowledge: critical social science has enlightenment and emancipation as goals, and it integrates critique and action, theory and practice. Carr and Kemmis (1986) apply these methodologies specifically to education, describing a "critical education science" (p. 156). They describe a "view of educational reform that is participatory and collaborative" and "a form of educational research which is conducted by those involved in education themselves. . . . [C]ritical educational science is not research *on* or *about* education, it is research *in* and *for* education" (p. 156). In other words, educators develop their understanding of their practice by becoming researchers on their practice (see Chapter Seven for a description of action research). The process of critical self-reflection has the potential to lead to educator development which is transformative and emancipatory.

It is important to note, in summary, that all three forms of knowledge—instrumental, practical, and emancipatory—are valid and necessary for human progress. Habermas does not reject instrumental knowledge, but rather he criticizes its pervasive application to inappropriate domains. Our industrial, technological, and information-based societies have led us to believe that all knowledge can be defined from these interests. For adult educators, there is important instrumental knowledge, and we should not trivialize this. On the other hand, what we cannot do is to view all of learning about teaching as the acquisition of instrumental knowledge. Neither can we hold the expectation that the empirical-analytical research methodologies will yield the "truth" about effective education, which we can then just learn to do. Adult educator development is also subjective, personal, and critical.

Educator Development in Context

Regardless of the context within which educators work, there has been the tendency to view the development of practice as the improvement of technique or skill. Instructional development for the university or college instructor has focused on presentation skills or better questioning techniques. Faculty have tended to use quantitative measurement of students' perceptions of their teaching as a means of determining which skills to work on. Educators whose discipline lies in the sciences or even the social sciences (emulating the sciences) are familiar with and respect instrumental knowledge as true and valid and will naturally apply those methods to understanding teaching.

For trainers in business and industry, where the content of their training may often be technical skills, there is also a tendency to see training as another technical skill. Development of trainers' practice may be seen to be the improvement of the sessions' objectives or the development of a better analysis of the task. The journal *Training and Development*, for example, presents a mostly technical perspective. There is a growing literature on transformation in the workplace (Watkins and Marsick, 1993; Wellins, Byham, and Wilson, 1991), but change in practice is not without difficulty. In their discussion of one such case, Watkins and Marsick (1993, p. 123) say how "intensely difficult such change is for organizations now rigidly hierarchical."

Educators in the health professions seem to be especially interested in the development of their practice. However, they are influenced in their perceptions, as would be expected, by the medical model. In the medical field, instrumental knowledge is strongly valued. Medical researchers are critical of interpretive research paradigms in which patients are asked to describe their experiences related to treatment. The improvement of practice involves scientifically determining the best method for teaching skills, knowledge, or problem solving (for example, see Dolmans, Gijselaers, Schmidt, and Van Der Meer, 1993). Although she is writing about professional education in general rather than only in the health professions, Cavanaugh (1993) is especially critical of the scientific and technical approach. She acknowledges the importance of knowledge acquisition but argues strongly against its pervasiveness in curricula.

In community education, practitioners tend to be part-time and identify with their full-time occupation rather than with education. Apps (1994) discusses the development of new perspectives in community or continuing education. The metaphors are changing, he writes. "The old metaphors of assembly lines and factories, of sports and the military, are declining. New metaphors of journeys, of dances, and of butterflies unfolding are emerging, along with a host of other metaphors not yet identified but implying cooperation, renewal of the spirit, and individual and organizational transformation" (p. 172). He envisions the new educator as teaching with the heart as well as with the mind, teaching to refresh the spirit as well as challenge the mind. At present, in community education practice, the teachers are less visible and their development more neglected. Apps's inspirational writing can provide us with a goal to change that perspective.

The educators who work in informal settings may be the least likely to see themselves as educators. They are also the people who are most likely to be working in the domain of emancipatory learning. They are informal leaders, activists, change agents, people with a vision of how things could be. As adult education changes in its perspective from "a mechanistic attitude marked by objectivity, control, predictability, competition, efficiency, and single views of knowledge to an attitude that values context, shared power, multiple relationships, and varied knowledge sources" (Apps, 1994, p. 18), adult educators who work outside of the formal organizational settings will need to be drawn into our discussions of educator development.

Adult educator development involves increasing instrumental, practical, and emancipatory knowledge. In practice, the emphasis is on increasing instrumental knowledge, regardless of the educators' context. Kincheloe (1991, p. 94) writes: "Because the public was impressed with the trappings of hard science and business terminology, educational leaders were rewarded for devoting most of their efforts to matters of efficiency and measurement. No matter how hard it may be, administrative theorists argued, it is necessary for educational leaders to establish quantifiable standards in the intangible as well as the more concrete fields of study. In this way educational leaders could improve their public images because it would be possible to report research on educational progress in comparative numerical terminology which everyone could understand." Educators want to be able to say, "I achieved 3.12 last year and I achieved 3.42 this year, so I have clearly improved." Educator development has focused on this expectation, thereby neglecting practical and emancipatory learning. I will elaborate on this in

Chapter Two. The emphasis on instrumental knowledge in educator development is not a fault of educators, but rather a product of the pervasiveness of the scientific ideology. We all use the words "scientific" or "objective" to comment positively on the validity of something we hear or read.

Summary

Who are adult educators? How are we prepared for our educator roles? What kinds of things do we do to develop our practice? What kinds of knowledge and learning do we see as relevant to our development? The answers to these questions are not simplistic. I have provided a brief overview in this chapter.

Adult educators work in a bewildering array of contexts. This diversity makes it difficult to draw together any one description of adult education practice and has been used as a rationale for the lack of development of a theory or framework for adult education. I have described six settings out of the many that exist: universities, colleges, business and industry, health professions, community education, and informal settings. The common theme that runs through these descriptions is that the educators identify more with their discipline, subject area, trade, or profession than they do with education. In most areas, instrumental knowledge of the content is regarded as the important learning to be delivered to students.

In the recent literature, and especially with the influence of Habermas's writing on the educational literature, we have come to see that technical interests and instrumental knowledge are not adequate to understand our practice. Instrumental knowledge is concerned with the prediction and control of our environment and the delineation of cause-and-effect relationships. It is rare that this knowledge is relevant to the complexities of educational practice. Practical knowledge, the knowledge of social norms, traditions, and values underlying our culture, and a mutual understanding of individuals forms a large part of our knowledge of our practice. Gaining practical knowledge can be viewed as a major component of educator development. However, it may be emancipatory knowledge, individuals' self-knowledge and social knowledge, which is crucial to educator development. Critical self-reflection leads to emancipatory knowledge. Mezirow's (1991) concept of transformative learning is based on Habermas's notion of emancipatory knowledge.

It is no surprise that adult educator development in the various contexts is viewed as the increase in technical knowledge of the subject area or of teaching itself. There is little reason to believe that adult educators see their development as being in the domain of practical (communicative) learning or emancipatory learning. This, I believe, is why we need to take a new approach to development for educators. This is what I discuss in Chapter Two.

If we see educator development as a process of transformative learning, then we gain a fresh perspective on what it means to learn about our practice.

Chapter Two

Traditional Developmental Strategies

Traditionally, developmental strategies for educators focused on the improvement of skills and the acquisition of new knowledge and techniques. Although these activities are an essential part of professional development, the recent emphasis in the adult education literature on critical reflection and transformative learning gives us new insights into how educators learn. If adults learn by transforming their perspectives (Mezirow, 1991) or by reconstructing their experiences (Tennant and Pogson, 1995), then we should be able to apply our understanding of these processes to learning about educational practice. We can integrate our learning into our practice—learn about teaching while we are teaching—and reconstruct what we know in addition to acquiring new knowledge.

At the end of a day of organizing and leading training seminars, the trainer goes to an adult education course at the local university and discusses in small groups the meaning of self-directed learning. After a busy spring spent running the performance appraisal system in the department, the human resource developer goes to a conference retreat to learn about innovative techniques in the field. When the semester is over and the final grades submitted, the college instructor is invited to a series of professional development workshops on planning courses and constructing tests.

Thus although a lot of our learning takes place apart from doing, we know that "learning by doing," or learning from experience, is critical. What we tend to do is incorporate learning-by-doing activities into learning experiences that are actually isolated from the workplace or the rest of the life of the learner and hope that they can be transferred back to practice. This does happen, of course, but many factors can interfere, including the culture of the educator's organization.

Professional preparation schools are grounded in a model of education that separates learning from doing, and this way of thinking has been carried into professional development experiences as well. In our childhood education, we perceived schools as the place of learning; we went to school in a separate building at predetermined times of the day and year. When school was over, learning was finished. Professional education (for teachers, nurses, social workers, and the like) is largely conducted by colleges and universities outside of the schools, hospitals, and social service agencies, even though practice teaching, clinical experiences, and fieldwork are inserted into the programs. Trades training comes closer to incorporating on-the-job experiences directly into the program, but the isolated school component remains the determining factor in learners' success at the trade; it is here that the evaluation takes place. The German apprenticeship model (Wilson, 1992) is well known for its learning-on-the-job philosophy, but still, "[t]he dual system is a combination of practical and theoretical vocational training at two places of learning with different legal and structural characteristics: in-plant and in-school training" (p. 33). It is not my intent here to argue that our preparatory systems are wrong, but rather to demonstrate that our thinking about educator development naturally follows from our experiences of preparatory education, in which learning was mostly isolated from practice.

In describing learning about work, Jarvis (1992b) reminds us that there are two forms of experience: primary and secondary. "The latter involves experiences in which interaction or teaching occurs over and above the primary experience. Hence, in the workplace there can be two simultaneous experiences: that which the workers are experiencing and that skill that they are being taught in a human resource development or continuing professional education program" (Jarvis, 1992b, pp. 180–181). Marsick and Watkins (1990) describe the learning that takes place from primary experience in the workplace as incidental or unintended. In Schön's (1983) work, professionals are described as learning during their practice (through reflection-in-action), but it is acknowledged that this process may not be viewed as learning by the professionals themselves.

With this background in mind, I review traditional developmental strategies. I examine each strategy in terms of the likelihood of its leading to the types of knowledge presented in Chapter One, and I analyze each in relation to its congruence with practice. I argue that frequently our developmental strategies emphasize instrumental knowledge and take place separately from actual practice. If we can also critically examine our practice in its own context, we can further enhance development.

I have selected for discussion some of the most commonly used developmental strategies: manuals, guides, newsletters, and how-to books; workshops; retreats; training programs; and evaluations and performance appraisals. I have deliberately excluded individual consultation between developer and educator, as its nature is unique to the people involved and it is difficult to make generalizable comments.

Manuals, Guides, Newsletters, and How-To Books

What does a professional do when in doubt? Search for an answer or a suggestion in print. Human resource developers, instructional developers, training consultants, and nursing educators often turn to printed materials for the answers to educational problems. Consequently, we have seen a proliferation of how-to materials for educators over the last three or four decades. Imel (1991, p. 15) is prompted to write: "The task of keeping up with the professional literature in adult education may create information anxiety. Rapid expansion of the field's literature base makes it difficult to keep abreast of the latest publications as well as to evaluate their relevance to any ongoing work."

The expectation that we can turn to a manual to find a solution to an educational problem, in much the same way that we turn to a computer manual to find out why the machine does not behave as we want, may be rooted in our perception of what a profession is. For the last three hundred years, Western thought has been shaped by the rise of science and technology. It has been our belief that through technical rationality, we could cure the ills of the world. Traditionally, professions have been defined in terms of the extent to which they utilize technical rationality, or instrumental knowledge, as described in Chapter One. In an important book on the professions, Moore (1970, p. 56) wrote that a profession "involves the application of general principles to specific problems, and it is a feature of modern sciences that such general principles are abundant and growing." Glazer (1974) distinguished between major or "near-major" professions—such as medicine, law, business, and engineering—and minor professions—such as social work, education, and town planning—on the basis of technical rationality. The minor professions are described as being unable to develop a base of scientific knowledge. The knowledge base of a real profession is seen to be specialized, firmly bounded, scientific, and standardized.

The conceptualization of professional knowledge as being best learned through reflection on practice (as described by Cervero, 1989; Harris, 1993) has not been at the core of definitions of a profession.

Education wants to be a major profession, or at least a near-major profession. What better way than to strive for general principles that can be applied to specific problems? Thus, we have what Stubblefield (1991) describes as the procedural literature in adult education. He writes: "Adult education as a procedural discipline provides guidelines for practice, and its literature is prescriptive" (p. 28), and "Beyond prescriptions for effective practice lies a more generic question about the nature of professional practice itself" (p. 29). It seems that we hope to define ourselves as professionals by being able to provide clear-cut answers to educational problems.

Type of Knowledge

An examination of manuals, guides, newsletters, and how-to books supports the notion that we hope to have an instrumental knowledge base in adult education. Indeed, there may well be aspects of our practice that can be described in terms of cause and effect. As an example, we may accept that continuous and ongoing feedback is conducive to learning and that perhaps this is a generic principle of effective education. However, even this principle can be questioned. Do all learners benefit from continuous feedback? What kind of feedback? Are there times when feedback is inappropriate?

As one illustration, in the procedural literature we find Pisk-urich (1993, pp. 64–65) writing, "I'm not going to go too deeply here into the *correct* way to write objectives. There are plenty of books on the subject, and in all honesty, I don't think there is one correct way. . . . However, there are three rules for the writing of objectives for self-directed learning materials that I think are inviolable." He then identifies the three rules: write objectives for the trainees, use performance-based verbs (a list of appropriate verbs is provided), and use a valid job analysis.

There are dozens of examples of books, manuals, and guides on how to be a better educator. Many, of which Piskurich's book is one example, demonstrate our desire to know how to do things right. We do need to have our own rules and procedures, and beginning educators acquire this knowledge from books as well as the other developmental strategies. However, as we continue to grow and develop as educators we often begin to question those rules, to reconstruct our experience, and to reconsider our assumptions. The "how-to" manuals no longer meet our changing learning needs.

Congruence with Practice

Educators rarely think of or describe their practice as being predictable, regulated, or explained by rules and principles. Every professional developer knows the common reaction to a suggested technique: "Oh, that won't work with my group," followed by a description of the content, the learners, or the organization. Every educator sees her or his teaching context as unique, and indeed it is.

Brookfield (1990a, p. 1) describes teaching as a complex and passionate experience: "Passion, hope, doubt, fear, exhilaration, weariness, colleagueship, loneliness, glorious defeats, hollow victories, and above all, the certainties of surprise and ambiguity—how can one begin to capture the reality of teaching in a single word or phrase." He goes on to say, "The idiosyncratic messiness of classroom reality is . . . far removed from the orderly textbook version (in which teachers carefully apply systematic methods in the pursuit of unequivocal objectives)." Some days a strategy will work, the classroom will be alive with conversation, activity, and interested learners; the next day or the next week the same strategy can yield blank stares or the glazed-over eyes indicating boredom. In the same group, one individual can love a visualization technique, another feels that it is a personal intrusion, and several others feel silly but try anyway. I consider myself to be a good educator generally, but some days I simply have no idea what went wrong. When I ask the group, they may say, "It has nothing to do with you; we're upset about what happened to Shirley yesterday," or perhaps, "We're just tired of group work tonight." The how-to book cannot include these irregularities.

Schön (1983, 1987) approaches this issue from a slightly different angle. He argues that we intuitively make decisions about our practice while we are practicing. He describes teaching as an art, not a set of skills or techniques. In fact, he argues that viewing teaching, or other professional practice, as technical expertise limits our potential for reflection: "Many practitioners, locked into a view of themselves as technical experts, find nothing in the world of practice to occasion reflection. They have become too skillful at techniques of selective inattention, junk categories, and situational control, techniques which they use to preserve the constancy of their knowledge-in-practice. For them, uncertainty is a threat; its admission is a sign of weakness" (Schön, 1983, p. 69).

Recent research into teachers' thinking and knowledge about teaching in the public school setting supports the notion that educators recognize the complexity of their practice (Hargreaves and Fullan, 1992; Russell and Munby, 1992), or, as Brookfield calls it, "the chaos" (1990a, p. 1). New educators also describe their practice as ambiguous and unpredictable (for example, see Eble, 1988). In the face of the complex nature of our practice, it is natural to seek guidelines and principles to restore order. Teaching tips and guidelines perform this function well and are especially useful for new educators as a starting point. But they cannot be congruent with practice because they cannot take into account the almost infinite variations in what we do. Sometimes, a belief in the expert's advice may even lead us to a sense of insecurity, as we try to implement the expert's sure-fire formula and see that it does not turn out.

Many educators who call or drop into the office of a human resource developer or faculty developer want a quick answer. They may ask for a handout on how to increase learner participation or how to hold more effective staff meetings. Understandably, people expect a professional developer to have answers. If not, can he or she be considered an expert or a professional? The developer, of course, accepts the client's request and often works from there to encourage reflection. Perhaps what we also need to do is change the focus in our materials. Manuals, guides, newsletters, and books can emphasize critical questioning, reflection, and the "chaos" of educator practice, as does, for example, Brookfield's (1990a) *The Skillful Teacher.*

Workshops

Workshops may well be the most common professional development activity. In an early literature review on the improvement of teaching in higher education, Levinson-Rose and Menges (1981) noted that workshops were the most common faculty development format and, further, that the only evaluation of their effectiveness was participant satisfaction ratings. Workshops tend to be one-half or one-day sessions, though they may be as short as one hour or as long as several days. Generally, they focus on techniques or strategies, such as how to adopt an appropriate leadership style, write objectives, assess performance, ask questions, or improve relations with staff.

As the label *workshop* implies, these sessions are meant to include experiential or hands-on learning. The original meaning of the term was a room or building in which work, especially mechanical work, was carried on. We now tend to use the term to describe a session that emphasizes the exchange of ideas and the demonstration and application of techniques and skills. Some workshops lean toward lectures or presentations, with a token group activity thrown in to justify the title.

The literature on workshops is mostly from the 1970s (for example, see Davis, 1974) and addresses the practicalities of conducting good sessions. Zuber-Skerritt (1992, p. 178) describes workshops as "ideal for discussion in small, leaderless groups." She discusses the advantages of one-time workshops in which staff can be introduced to a topic or problem which they are specifically interested in, but she points out that an integrated series of workshops allows for more in-depth and individualized discussion. Zuber-Skerritt also emphasizes that the skill of the workshop leader is critical to the success of the session, a point that can hardly be argued. It is interesting that she refers to what could be a description of transformative learning: "The process of 'unfreezing' old behaviour, trying out alternative behaviours and arriving at new, improved, deliberate and controlled action must be at the core of all PD [professional development] workshops if they are to effect real change" (p. 180).

Type of Knowledge

By definition, the workshop format is intended for the attainment and practice of techniques and skills. The format is derived from the carpenter's or the auto mechanic's workshop where tradespeople learn how to use their tools and equipment. When it follows this tradition, the workshop emphasizes instrumental knowledge.

A typical workshop might include the following agenda items: introductions and an ice-breaker in which participants get to know each other and state their expectations of the session; a short presentation by the workshop leader on the topic; a group activity in which participants apply the concepts to their practice; a reporting back by the small groups and a general discussion of their work; and a summary and integration by the workshop leader. Sometimes, longer sessions repeat this cycle as often as the time allows. This format follows the original notion of "workshop" in which learners might be introduced to a new piece of equipment, have a chance to try it out, and report back to the instructor on their experiences.

Workshops in the social sciences have evolved and are considered useful by both educators and developers. Dirkx, Lavin, Spurgin, and Holder (1993), for example, report on educators' perceptions of continuing education workshops and conclude that the participants' expectations of helpful activities were consistent with the practical perspective of continuing education. Of course, there is a tremendous diversity of workshop formats and styles, and generalizations do not hold true for every workshop. Often in education, practical or communicative knowledge is emphasized. The use of group work and discussion fosters communication among individuals and a sharing of their experiences. Such activities can stimulate emancipatory or transformative learning, especially when the workshop is held over time in an integrated-series format.

Congruence with Practice

In a discussion of traditional instructional development activities in higher education, Amundsen, Gryspeerdt, and Moxness (1993, p. 329) comment that "techniques were taught and evaluated in isolation without any attempt to fit them into the wider context of the teaching-learning process or within the professor's existing knowledge of instruction." Similarly, in a discussion of the preparation of professionals, where workshops are often used, Cavanaugh (1993) describes the discontinuity of education and practice. Although professional development workshops vary greatly across contexts, they have some common characteristics that could be related to their becoming isolated from practice. The workshop is often planned in advance of the leader's meeting the participants. It may be advertised or promoted throughout an organization or professional association. People then choose to attend based on the description of the workshop, a description that is designed to attract participants. Even though every good workshop leader asks participants what their expectations are at the beginning of a session, it is difficult to change an agenda if people's needs are very different from what has been planned. In this case, congruence with practice depends on the accuracy of the advertising and the reasons people had for deciding to attend.

When the group is more homogeneous, such as in a workshop for one department of an organization or for, say, literacy volunteers, it is more likely that the content will be congruent with the participants' practice. This depends in part on the degree to which the workshop leader is familiar with the educators' context and expectations, and in part on the kind of preplanning that is done. For example, if participants are involved in the planning, and if the agenda remains open to change as the workshop progresses, congruence can increase.

Retreats

Retreats are sessions held away from the educators' normal workplace. They tend to be of a longer duration than workshops, and they often include some social activities in addition to the discussions, presentations, and group work. Retreats may be organized by one organization or institution for their educators or trainers; they may be organized by professional associations or more informal groups and thus be available to participants from different organizations. Some retreats precede or follow professional conferences.

The formats that retreats can take vary widely. They may have a specific topic or theme; they may be brainstorming, needs-assessment, or problem-solving sessions; they may be wide-open discussion groups; or they can involve practical, experiential learning of a new method or medium, such as a computer technology. One advantage that retreats have over workshops is their longer duration, and hence their potential to foster critical reflection. A second advantage is that participants are away from the routines and distractions of their usual practice. A retreat will stand out as a special event, and the learning may, by association, also stand out in participants' subsequent reflection on their practice. There is no guarantee, of course, of particular kinds of learning occurring at a retreat; as with any session this depends on the purpose, the participants, the facilitators or leaders, and the nature of follow-up events.

Although retreats are a common professional development approach, there is little literature on their content, style, or effectiveness. Selman and Dampier (1991, p. 137) discuss the general advantages of residential centers for learning, commenting that "there are numerous such centres across Canada, and all exhibit the same support for learning." The authors do not provide further details. One example that I am familiar with is the Niagara Institute, a nonprofit organization that offers three-day retreats for managers from business, industry, and government. The retreat is described as a "proven program to develop the attitudes, techniques and strategies required to be the new kind of leader" (Niagara Institute, 1994, p. 1). It is promoted as "interweaving theory, practical information, discussion, personal reflection and action planning to create a life-changing experience" (p. 1).

For university educators, an example of the use of retreats can be found in the Lilly Teaching Fellows Program, which includes, among other components, spring weekend conferences held at different sites throughout the eastern United States. Austin (1992) conducted a survey of participants in this program, interviewed selected faculty, and made site visits to assess the effectiveness of the program. Austin found that participants' "personal teaching philosophies expanded as they read the research literature related to teaching" (p. 95) and included quotations from faculty about "philosophical shifts." Participants also mentioned learning about instructional methods and design, confidence building, and increased commitment to teaching as among the benefits of the program.

Type of Knowledge

Retreats have the potential to foster critical reflection if the activities, discussions, or group work are designed with that goal in mind. However, if a retreat is a one- or two-day event, with no follow-up activities, the likelihood of its leading to sustained critical reflection may decrease. Mezirow describes what a program designed to foster communicative learning would help learners do:

Decontextualize

Become aware of the history, contexts, and consequences of their beliefs

Become more reflective and critical

"Bracket" preconceived ideas

Make better inferences, more appropriate generalizations, and more logically coherent arguments

Be more open to the perspectives of others

Rely less on psychological defense mechanisms (Mezirow, 1991, p. 215)

In addition, transformative learning includes a critique of the premises that need reassessment and a revision of distorted assumptions or values. This is a difficult bill to fill in a one-time session, even if it is of several days' duration.

I argue, nevertheless, that a retreat format for development work could be a good starting point for emancipatory learning. Decontextualization, self-awareness, bracketing of ideas, and critical questioning would be enhanced by being away from the workplace. In the process of working toward transformative learning, the individual needs to step outside of himself or herself—examine long-held beliefs through different eyes or from a fresh perspective. A change in environment and an intensive focus on one's practice could enhance such an effort. In the three-day retreat offered by the Niagara Institute mentioned earlier, the managers are staying and working in an attractive rural setting usually quite distant from their workplace. They engage in an assessment of their leadership style, psychological type, communication skills, and career goals as a part of the retreat. The combination of self-assessment and distance from work has the potential to stimulate critical self-reflection and transformation. If the process is continued rather than treated as an isolated event, emancipatory development could occur.

Congruence with Practice

The degree to which the retreat format for developmental work is congruent with educators' practice depends on the design and the activities included. By its very nature, the retreat is isolated from practice in the way that a workshop is, or perhaps even more so. On the other hand, the longer time available allows the use of strategies such as simulations, critical incidents, role play, and case studies, all of which can be designed to bring in problems, experiences, and issues from participants' practice. Mezirow (1991, p. 214) warns us, though, that simply bringing in role plays does not necessarily foster communicative learning about one's practice: "The assumption seems to be that these things are learned in much the same way as any other behavioral skill except that practice occasionally requires the use of hypothetical reality contexts such as role playing, which are unnecessary in learning to operate a lathe or perform other manual tasks."

In my experience, retreats generate considerable enthusiasm about making changes to practice—often committees and task forces are set up at the end of a retreat to implement new ideas. However, participants may then return to the workplace, comment for a few days or even weeks about what a good retreat they had, and gradually lose sight of the insights and plans they had made. The retreat can be a stimulating experience, but the nature of the work and the culture of the organization to which the educators return can separate the learning from practice. If the developmental activities are a part of actual practice, this separation cannot occur as easily.

Training Programs

Training programs for educators are found primarily in business and industry and are often referred to as "train-the-trainer" programs. Sometimes government departments and health professionals also use this approach to educator development. Programs for training the trainer vary significantly in their approach, content, and duration, as do workshops and retreats. They have, though, some underlying assumptions in common which warrant special treatment here.

In writing about the "art of managing," Schön (1983) makes comments that are equally relevant to trainers in organizations: "The field of management has long been marked by a conflict between two competing views of professional knowledge. On the first view, the manager is a technician whose practice consists in applying to the everyday problems of his organization the principles and methods derived from management science. On the second, the manager is a craftsman, a practitioner of an art of managing that cannot be reduced to explicit rules and theories" (pp. 236–237). He notes that the "first view has gained steadily in power" (p. 237).

Traditional train-the-trainer programs tend to view the trainer as a technician. Mager (1962) is the father of this perspective; it is one that has generated an enormous literature on systematic, objectives-based approaches to training. As I discussed in Chapter One, training itself is generally based on the underlying assumption that problems in an organization are caused by knowledge or skill deficits that can be remedied through instrumental learning. As can be expected, this model is also applied to learning about training. One example is Bard, Bell, Stephen, and Webster's *The Trainer's Professional Development Handbook* (1987). This book contains a directory of learning aids and materials as well as specific guidelines on how to develop learning plans to increase professional competence.

Wilson (1992) provides some examples of train-the-trainer programs. They range in nature from twelve- to fifteen-week courses to one-day sessions. Examples of the topics are the concepts, principles, and techniques of assessing training and development needs; design and delivery of effective training programs; the role and scope of government-funded training programs; and effective training strategies for coping with technological change. Programs are offered by in-house trainers, training managers, private practitioners, or professional associations. Wilson (1992, p. 55) describes the offerings as "outcome-oriented, pragmatic and issue-specific, rather than general in nature."

Type of Knowledge

Technical interests are expressed through the medium of work. Carr and Kemmis (1986) describe instrumental knowledge as necessary for modern industry and production processes, and as "scientific explanation" (p. 134). It is not surprising therefore that many training programs for educators in business, industry, hospitals, and government agencies focus on instrumental knowledge. The systems within which trainers work have technical interests. The goal of the organization is to maintain the most efficient and effective outcomes. Trainers are often individuals who have worked in other aspects of the organization before taking on a trainer's role; they bring the goals and values of the organization's culture with them.

On the other hand, many programs that retain the label "train the trainer" have moved away from the technical approach. With the increased emphasis on teamwork, empowerment, and participative decision making (see Watkins and Marsick, 1993, for example), a strictly technical approach is no longer seen as valid. At times, though, concepts such as the-worker-as-decision-maker are used as rhetoric aimed at increasing labor productivity rather than at meaningful change in training (Wells, 1987).

The design of training programs may be driven by the notion that in a given situation there is an appropriate technique to be applied that will lead to people obtaining pre-determined knowledge or skills. Ewert (1991, p. 350) writes: "With student achievement as the objective, the instrumental approach focuses on tools, resources, environments, techniques, teachers, and students as the means to that given end. Education systems are viewed as an input-output system, where resources and raw materials enter at one end and the finished product, an achieving 'educated' student, issues from the other. Within this delivery system, educational problems are viewed as blockages, caused by inappropriate teacher behaviors, student inadequacies, or inefficient resource uses." As Watkins and Marsick (1993) advocate, training can be redesigned to encourage continuous learning based on a partnership among executives, human resource developers, and managers.

Congruence with Practice

It may be the emphasis on instrumental knowledge in some organizations that maintains the congruence between trainers' development and their view of their practice. If "human performance technology" (Butler Research Associates, 1989) is the new and emerging focus for trainers, it is also likely that they view the development of their own practice in the same way. "The new human performance technology assumes that the purpose of training is to improve job performance and, more importantly, to impact on the organization's bottom line (be it dollars, service, or reputation). Performance technology's aim, then, is not to provide training nor merely to improve performance, it is to make a positive contribution to the outcome of the organization" (Geis, 1991, p. 16). With this as the purpose of training, the goal of training the trainer will be to increase that person's performance in getting others to have an impact on the organization's bottom line. This leads to congruence between development and practice for the trainer, as long as the underlying approach of instrumental learning is not questioned.

Many programs for trainers are designed to keep the content and activities congruent with trainers' practice. Some graduate-level programs even have a curriculum that reflects the instrumental approach. To give one example, the core courses of Concordia University's Ph.D. program in Educational Technology are Instructional Design, Human Resources Development, Research Methods and Practices, Educational Cybernetics, Systems Analysis and Design, Theory, Development and Research in Educational Media, Distance Education, and Thesis Research. Other programs, of course, take a more developmental and nonlinear approach (as examples, the University of Texas at Austin and the University of Calgary's continuing education master's degree).

As I discussed earlier, workshops and retreats can be isolated from educators' practice by virtue of their being held at the end of the day or away from the workplace. This is also true of many train-the-trainer programs, especially those where the trainers go to a university, college, or professional association center. It could be that the specific information and activities are not directly related to individuals' practice even though the underlying philosophy may be in tune with the trainers' approach. In-house training programs are less likely to create this schism between content and practice.

When trainers encounter programs based on a different perspective, they can experience a dramatic conflict between their practice and the program. To illustrate this, I describe Bob, who enrolled in a seminar in adult education last year.

Bob is a trainer in a government department. In the group of twenty-five, there were three other self-described trainers, one from the health professions, one from private industry, and one from an entrepreneurship center at a college. It was Bob who most strongly felt the discrepancy between his practice and the content of the seminar. He initially stated his goal for the seminar as being "to obtain better facilitation skills." As we read, discussed, and worked with the concepts of self-directed learning, personal autonomy, critical reflection, and transformative learning, Bob devoted his energies to drawing specific skills and techniques out of the content and the process. He would often ask others in the group what technique they would use in a situation. He was interested in why the facilitator was doing what she was doing, and he observed her closely. This served Bob well for the first semester. He simply extracted what he could, while considering the theoretical discussions not relevant to his work.

We did not expect Bob back for the second semester, but he arrived. This time it was not as easy for him. As the group discussed and planned the topics they wanted to work with during the seminar, it was clear that Bob's voice was almost unheard. Over the semester, he gradually withdrew, attending more and more infrequently, choosing to find things to read on his own that better suited his goals. Some weeks later, Bob told me that he had had difficulty trying to reconcile the discrepancy between his perspective of training and others' perspectives of education.

Evaluations and Performance Appraisals

There can be no question that evaluation of educators' performance has been the most common entry into developmental activities over the past three decades. In a recent edited volume, Banta and Associates (1993) provide a comprehensive overview of the impact that evaluation has had on teaching in higher education. Theall and Franklin (1991) dedicate one-third of their *Effective Practices for Improving Teaching* to evaluation. Centra (1993, p. 19) argues that "[e]valuation can play an important role in developing teaching effectiveness" and presents a model for enhancing teaching through formative evaluation.

In higher education, students' ratings of teaching are the most common form of evaluation. An extensive literature addresses the reliability and validity of student ratings; many scholars dedicate their careers to the study of this form of evaluation; Centra (1993) provides a good recent summary of this research. Other formats for the evaluation of educators' practice are encouraged in most institutions but used much less frequently. For example, faculty sometimes use peer review of their course materials, others' (peers, instructional developers, or administrators) observations of their teaching, videotape analyses, interviews or discussions with students, input from professional organizations, or follow-up studies of how alumni perceived their courses.

In business, industry, government, and health-professional organizations, *performance appraisal* is the term most often used for evaluation of individuals' practice (Robbins and Stuart-Kotze, 1994). Rating scales are also commonly used, but not to the extent that they are used in higher education. Ratings are given by staff, peers, or supervisors. Other methods include written essays or reports; critical incidents, which focus on critical behaviors that separate effective from ineffective performance; and multiperson comparisons, in which individuals are ranked or ordered in comparison to others' performance (Robbins and Stuart-Kotze, 1994).

The emphasis on rating scales for evaluation comes from the belief that quantitative data are more objective and more precise. It is based on the assumption that educators' practice can be measured empirically. I witnessed an extreme example of this approach in an organization in which ratings were averaged across items, giving each educator one number to describe their effectiveness. People would receive an overall average rating of 2.82 or 3.24. Part-time people, hired on contract for specific programs or sessions, were then rank-ordered according to this number, and those on the bottom were not rehired regardless of the absolute value of the number or the size of the difference between their number and another person's number.

In all settings, evaluations are conducted both to provide feedback to the individual (formative evaluation) and to make administrative decisions (summative evaluation), although I have argued elsewhere (Cranton, 1993) that this distinction is not a useful one for educators to make. It is possible to view all evaluation of educator practice as developmental, except in cases where evaluation procedures are abused, as in the example given in the preceding paragraph. It is rare that real administrative decisions are made based on evaluation results: even the promotion and tenure process in higher education can be viewed as developmental. Nevertheless, when the formative-summative distinction is made, it is formative evaluation that is linked to educator development, as one would expect. This link is so strong that some human resource developers have performance appraisal as their major responsibility, and some instructional development centers in higher education dedicate the majority of their time to conducting evaluations. The expectation is that when people receive feedback on their practice, they will be moved to make changes in areas where the feedback is negative. Early behavioral approaches to teacher education (for example, Gage, 1977) followed this model. Microteaching, a technique in which teacher trainees are videotaped conducting short instructional segments, remains a popular strategy. Yet there is resistance to this kind of developmental work. This is perhaps because, as Centra (1993, p. 11) states, "Most information, whether from students or from colleagues, is long on judgment and short on helpful advice." It is also because educators receiving feedback about their practice do not necessarily know how to change. If learners tell me that the organization of my courses is poor, how do I know what to do to change that? It is easier to blame the learners for not having the intelligence to see what organization I used, or blame the institution for requiring that I cover too much material in one course. Despite the good intentions, many results from evaluations or performance appraisals are filed and forgotten.

Type of Knowledge

Evaluation has the potential to lead to communicative or emancipatory learning about educator practice. Communicative learning could be fostered through the collection of qualitative information about practice, that is, through critical incidents, open-ended written or verbal comments from learners or peers, or reflective self-evaluation in a journal or log. Emancipatory or transformative learning could be stimulated through ongoing discussions with learners about the teaching and learning experience, or through extended discussions with a professional developer.

The most common format for evaluation of educator practice is the rating scale. Most rating scales focus on specific behaviors and skills. All rating scales, by definition, quantify people's perceptions of practice. Centra (1993, p. 176) writes: "For some psychometricians, it seems that an object or an effect does not exist unless it can be measured. Yet an old adage seems more applicable to many of life's phenomena: Not everything that counts can be counted and not everything that can be counted counts." Mezirow (1991) argues that if our goal "is to foster transformative learning, dogmatic insistence that learning outcomes be specified in advance of the educational experience in terms of observable changes in behavior or 'competencies' that are used as benchmarks against which to measure learning gains will result in a reductive distortion and serve merely as a device of indoctrination" (pp. 219–220). In other words, quantitative behavioral measures, such as rating scales, cannot be used to assess transformations in a person's perspective on practice. They are a means of determining learners' perceptions of the educator's observable behaviors.

Congruence with Practice

Last semester, I had two very different instructional development clients. By coincidence, I would frequently meet with them on the same day, heightening the contrast between them in my mind.

One client consistently presented me with student evaluations that were decidedly poor. On a 5-point scale, average ratings tended to be around 2. Open-ended comments were as devastating as "This is the worst teacher I've ever had" and "I don't know why this person is allowed to teach." The second client, on the same scale, received average ratings of over 4 on all items and had mostly rave reviews in the comments section of the form. The first client dismissed her results, claiming to be a good teacher and blaming the nature of her discipline for the learners' responses. The second client also dismissed his results, claiming that the learners were just being "nice." Perhaps the extent to which evaluations are congruent with practice is dependent both on the nature of the evaluation and the individual's perspective on his or her practice.

Evaluations that involve observation and discussion of teaching or analyses of videotapes of teaching are more likely to be or become congruent with educators' perspectives of their practice than are the results of rating scales. This is the rationale behind the use of microteaching, for example (Gage, 1977). It is harder to dismiss a videotape of yourself being domineering and aggressive than it is to dismiss a person's low rating of your interpersonal skills.

When evaluation is an interactive process with learners, the use of evaluation as a developmental strategy can become fully integrated with practice. An educator can collect open-ended comments from learners midway through a course or program, summarize these comments, make his or her comments in writing, and hold a discussion with the group about the meaning of the results, discrepancies between the learners' and the educator's views, and what kinds of changes could be made in the sessions. The same interactive process can be used in a performance appraisal process. In one such project (Cranton and Knoop, 1993), staff and managers are presented with information about evaluation in preparatory sessions. The sessions are interactive and provide the opportunity for people to discuss fears, anxieties, or other concerns about evaluation. Staff and sometimes peers provide ratings as well as open-ended comments; managers complete a self-evaluation. Each individual receives a report on the results, including numerical, narrative, and interpretive components. With the report, he or she receives guidelines such as how to hold a discussion with staff about the report and how to develop an action plan for change through interactions with staff. Managers then meet individually or in small groups with a consultant to discuss their results, how their own discussions with staff are proceeding, and their action plans. At this time they are also provided with printed materials on how to make changes in a variety of aspects of their practice. Human resource personnel, who previously saw evaluation as a "necessary evil" in their lives, began to see the process as being a part of their practice.

The connection between evaluations and other resources for development is another critical factor in determining how likely it is that evaluations will lead to change. As I mentioned earlier, it is one thing to be told by your learners that you are not well-organized. It is quite another to know what to do about it. If evaluation processes are linked with support systems, discussion groups, printed resources, or peer consultation programs, there is a higher likelihood that this strategy will be seen as congruent with educator practice.

When evaluations and performance appraisals are isolated from practice, they can fail to relate to our communicative and emancipatory interests. They become a routine requirement of an institution or organization, with little attention being paid to their results. When they are integrated into practice through discussions with learners and when they are linked to other resources for development, they can be a meaningful strategy.

Building on Traditional Developmental Strategies

I have been critical of traditional developmental strategies to the extent that they are focused solely on the acquisition of skills rather than encouraging critical reflection on practice and to the extent that they are separated from practice. Even new educators, who may benefit most from skills acquisition, also have many years of experience in educational systems (including being a learner) and learn through questioning their experiences. Nevertheless, it would be unfair to leave this chapter without drawing together and summarizing the characteristics of traditional strategies that provide meaningful experiences for educators. Regardless of whether we call something a workshop, a training session, or a retreat, the process can have potential for critical reflection. What are some characteristics that are needed for a professional development experience to be transformative?

- The inclusion of a variety of perspectives. Written materials can include alternative points of view; opposing theoretical positions can be presented and discussed in a retreat or workshop.
- The articulation of assumptions. The author of developmental materials and the training leader can make their own assumptions open as well as encourage participating educators to do the same.
- Discussion. Educators who talk to other educators and to their learners about their practice can clarify their own perspectives, receive support from others, and gain awareness of other points of view. Discussing the results of a performance appraisal with one's staff is one example; small-group interaction in a workshop is another.
- A critical attitude. We sometimes shun being critical, not wanting to be negative. But if critical questioning of what anyone says, including ourselves and including the experts, becomes a part of our developmental work, we can move away from our technical interests.
- Activities based on practice. When educators' own practice and experience is used in workshops, retreats, and training programs, there is a greater possibility of people using their learning to change their practice.

Summary

Commonly used development strategies for educators have been how-to materials, workshops, retreats, training programs, and evaluations and performance appraisals. Over the decades, there has been very little clear evidence that these strategies have a meaningful impact on practice. Possible reasons have been discussed in this chapter.

How-to books tend to be an expression of our hope that there is an instrumental-knowledge base in education. If only we can find the right technique and use it at the right time, we will become better educators. However, educators do not tend to see their actual practice as ordered and regulated by rules; the information in the how-to books may not be congruent with their perspective on practice unless it addresses the complexity of teaching. There is a societal value that objective and scientific knowledge is of more worth than dynamic, changing, or chaotic knowledge; this leads us to look for "truths" that may not exist.

Thousands of workshops are given somewhere every day, and there are good guidelines for designing workshops (Sork, 1984). Although they do not need to do so, often workshops tend to focus on the technical aspects of teaching. They can be isolated from practice, in part because of the type of knowledge conveyed and in part because they are usually held outside of working hours and the workplace.

Retreats have more potential than workshops to foster communicative or emancipatory learning, primarily because they are longer in duration and are usually conducted in an atmosphere conducive to reflection. Yet if there is little or no follow-up from a retreat, they can be regarded as an isolated event, apart from practice.

Train-the-trainer programs tend to be modeled on general training programs. Because they are connected with the world of business and industry, the "world of work," they traditionally represent people's technical interests: how can we increase the productivity of this organization? There are recent trends away from this perspective. The type of knowledge sought in train-the-trainer programs leads to congruence with trainers' perceptions of their practice. On the other hand, this perspective may not be the most appropriate for their own practice.

Evaluations and performance appraisals are commonly used as a starting point for educator development. Especially in higher education, considerable research has been done to address the usefulness and validity of student ratings of teaching. When evaluations are only quantitative in nature, they tend to emphasize educators' observable teaching behavior. However, evaluations and performance appraisals can take on many different formats, and when the educator is truly involved in understanding his or her practice through getting feedback from others and discussing that feedback with them, the process can be quite congruent with practice and can lead to communicative and emancipatory learning.

I have intended to argue in this chapter that we can enhance our developmental strategies by considering educators' communicative and emancipatory interests. In Chapters Three, Four, and Five, I view educator development from the perspective of adult learning: as an adult learner, the educator can draw from the theoretical work on self-directed learning, critical reflection, and transformative learning.

Chapter Three

Strategies for Self-Directed Development

Susan is a human resource developer in a large government department. She has learned about her practice primarily by working with a more experienced colleague, a woman she describes as her mentor. As time goes on, Susan begins to question some of the practices she and her colleague use. She thinks about trying different things. But Susan feels awkward bringing these ideas up with her colleague—she has always respected and followed in the footsteps of her mentor and worries that criticism would lead to resentment. When her colleague takes a maternity leave, Susan is both frightened and excited. Will she be able to carry out the work by herself? Can she use this time to experiment with alternative ideas? What if she fails?

Sometimes a person needs to be self-directed in order to reflect critically on practice. Sometimes becoming self-directed in one's practice is a transformation. Sometimes transformation is stimulated through the direction of another person but is in the end a self-directed process. Each of these alternatives could be the case for Susan.

I discuss self-directed learning before critical reflection and transformative learning not because there is a linear sequence to the process in learning—the concepts are interrelated in many ways—but rather because theoretically each concept builds on the previous one.

Independence, freedom, autonomy, empowerment, self-direction: in one form or another these have always been seen as the goals of human development and thus of education. Just as existentialist philosophers have struggled to define freedom (Macquarrie, 1973), so have adult educators struggled to define self-direction (Candy, 1991). The concept of self-direction has remained evasive. There is no common understanding among adult educators or scholars in adult education as to what they mean by self-direction. Yet this does not diminish its importance or the extent to which it has become a part of educators' espoused theories of practice. It would be rare to find an educator in Western culture who would not agree that he or she wanted learners to be more self-directed, more independent, or freer. These notions are an integral part of our social norms. Candy (1991, pp. 46–47) writes that self-direction "in the broadest sense seems to have captured the spirit of the times—that is, to embody a number of contemporary issues that have flowed together. These include the democratic ideal, the ideology of individualism, the concept of egalitarianism, the subjective or relativistic epistemology, the principles of humanistic education, and the construct of adulthood."

Educators are expected to be independent, self-directed professionals. We expect them to maintain an up-to-date expertise in their discipline, to initiate and implement innovations in their institution or organization, to contribute to their profession and their community, and to be responsible for their own professional development. However, as we saw in Chapter Two, traditional development strategies do not tend to encourage or even allow educators to have control over their own development. They may have a choice of which workshop to attend or which book to read, but it is often assumed that others know best what they need to learn.

If educator development is to be emancipatory or transformative, it is important that educators have control over their learning and access to the resources they need for learning. In Susan's case, she felt unable to transform her practice without having control, but she also would not have been able to do so without the experience she had gained with her mentor. These two criteria are used by Brookfield (1993) to define self-directed learning as a political concept. Simultaneously, the process of becoming a self-directed learner of one's practice may be transformative learning for educators. Susan's anxiety about being on her own could be the beginning of that process for her. If we are used to being told what we should do in order to work more effectively with our learners, and if we believe that our expertise lies in our subject area rather than in education, to change that perspective is transformative learning. This process is discussed in more detail in Chapter Five.

If educators see self-directed learning as a goal of their work with learners and do not see themselves as self-directed learners of educational practice, there is a discrepancy in their perspective. Mezirow (1991) describes perspective transformation as development. He writes, "transformation can lead developmentally toward a more inclusive, differentiated, permeable, and integrated perspective and that, insofar as it is possible, we all naturally move toward such an orientation. *This is what development means in adulthood* (emphasis in the original). It should be clear that a strong case can be made for calling perspective transformation the central process of adult development" (Mezirow, 1991, p. 155). Educators' professional development, when it moves beyond the acquisition of new techniques, is transformative learning. In order for this development to take place, educators need to develop as self-directed learners; this development, too, is transformative learning.

In this chapter, I first briefly review the variety of perspectives on self-directed learning, although it is not my intent to provide a full literature review. Candy (1991) and others do this well. I then use Candy's four dimensions of self-directed learning (1991) as a framework to discuss strategies for educators' development. He refers to "four distinct (but related) phenomena: 'self-direction' as a personal attribute (personal autonomy); 'self-direction' as the willingness and capacity to conduct one's own education (self-management); 'self-direction' as a mode of organizing instruction in formal settings (learner-control); and 'self-direction' as the individual noninstitutional pursuit of learning opportunities in the 'natural society setting' (autodidaxy)" (Candy, 1991, p. 23). Each of these phenomena is related to educator development as transformative learning.

Defining Self-Directed Learning

Jarvis (1992b, p. 130) notes that self-directed learning "is one of those amorphous terms that occurs in adult education literature but that lacks precise definition." Knowles (1975, 1980) introduced the term to practitioners, and his definition was pervasive in the literature until the late 1980s. His conceptualization follows an instructional design model, with the learners participating in or making the decisions. He saw self-directed learning as being a process in which learners "take the initiative, with or without the help of others" (1975, p. 18) in diagnosing their needs, setting objectives, selecting resources, choosing learning strategies, and evaluating their progress. Unfortunately, Knowles's work was misconstrued by researchers and practitioners alike. It was interpreted at times as independent learning, equivalent to modularized instruction or computer-managed instruction. Knowles actually emphasized people working together. Others assumed that adults were automatically self-directed, but Knowles had described their need or desire to take responsibility for their learning while acknowledging that people may not have the skills or the confidence to do so. What Knowles intended was similar to saying that people want to be free from constraints and oppression, but perhaps they are not or cannot be for various reasons.

During the 1980s, the concept of self-directed learning split into two related but conceptually different notions. It was seen as a characteristic of people, as in "She is a self-directed learner," and a method of learning, as in "He is using a self-directed approach in his course." The first concept, that of self-direction as a personal characteristic, led to researchers' attempts at quantification. Guglielmino's Self-Directed Learning Readiness Scale, or SDLRS (1977), and Oddi's Continuing Learning Inventory, or OCLI (1984), are two well-known examples of instruments designed to measure self-directedness. The SDLRS, in particular, has been used extensively in a variety of research studies (two of many examples are Long, 1987; and West and Bentley, 1989) and has provoked criticism and debate (Field, 1989). Three questions need to be considered regarding this line of inquiry:

1. What do such instruments measure?
2. Can self-directedness be quantified (which implies that it is instrumental knowledge)?
3. Can self-directedness be considered as a characteristic that is free of the learning and social context?

The second concept, that of self-directed learning as a method, led to the phenomenon of researchers conducting methods-comparison studies (for example, Rosenblum and Darkenwald, 1983). The learning and degree of satisfaction of participants who were and were not involved in the planning of learning were compared. This line of research resembled the 1960s experiments on the effectiveness of learner control (see Campbell, 1964). The early investigations of learner control generally revealed no measurable differences in learning as a result of method (Dubin and Taveggia, 1968). It is not surprising that comparing the self-directed learning "method" with other methods of instruction yields no meaningful results. Why would we expect groups of individuals, each with their distinct learner characteristics, experiences, and knowledge of and attitude toward the subject area, to respond predictably and consistently to being given responsibility for their own learning? As Candy (1991, p. 437) notes, "That such preoccupations are manifest in the literature on self-direction seems particularly ironic, in view of the nature of the phenomenon being studied."

Brookfield (1986) initiated the change in thinking about self-directed learning. He attempted to untangle the concepts of self-directedness as a measurable and assumed characteristic of adults, self-directed learning as a method, and self-directedness as an aim of education. He also questioned each of these assumptions. Candy (1991) then provided a thorough analysis of the various threads and dimensions of self-directed learning, drawing the factions together again into a four-faceted model. He argued against the positivistic approach to the study of self-directed learning, and consequently against attempts to measure self-directedness. In 1993, Brookfield clearly reconnected self-directed learning to the critical practice of adult education, or, in other words, emancipatory learning. He wrote, "The case for self-direction as an inherently political concept rests on two assumptions. First, that at the intellectual heart of self-direction is the issue of control, particularly control over what are conceived as acceptable and appropriate learning activities and processes. Second, that exercising self-direction requires that certain conditions be in place regarding access to resources, conditions that are essentially political in nature" (Brookfield, 1993, pp. 232–233).

At about the same time, Jarvis (1992b) attempted to "refine the notion of self-directed learning" by examining it through his analysis of "free will and freedom to act" (p. 131). He developed a model of self-directed learning in which he isolated nine major elements, seen as forming a variety of sequences of events shaping the learner's tendency to be self-directed or other-directed. The elements include

- Disjuncture, or discrepancy between past and present experience
- Decision to learn
- Type of participation, through an educational institution or independently
- Aims and objectives, whether they be determined by learners, others, or through negotiation
- Content, again whether it is determined by learners, others, or through negotiation
- Method
- Thought/language, a broad category including communicative interaction
- Assessment
- Action/outcome

Jarvis sees learners as being able to take various paths through each of these elements, being either self-directed or other-directed in each element.

Early in his writing, Mezirow (1985) described a self-directed learner as developing a more authentic meaning perspective, or in other words, engaging in critical self-questioning of underlying assumptions. He also related self-direction to the communicative aspect of transformative learning: "There is probably no such thing as a self-directed learner, except in the sense that there is a learner who can participate fully and freely in the dialogue through which we test our interests and perspectives against those of others and accordingly modify them and our learning goals" (Mezirow, 1985, p. 27).

Generally, self-directed learning has now been reintegrated with communicative learning and again seen to be a process concomitant with transformative learning. However, the branch of thinking in which self-direction is a quantifiable characteristic and a precise method remains in place. Long and his associates (1994) describe Brookfield's writing as the interjection of a "myth" into the literature. Long (1994, pp. 2) writes, "Unfortunately, the critical mythology continues to persist with little critical analysis" and "It is even more critical, however, when these myths are accepted to such a degree that they interfere with the development of research and practice. The myth gradually must be replaced with corrective information" (pp. 2–3). Piskurich's recent guide (1993) to the design and implementation of self-directed learning provides another example of this approach.

In an earlier book, I described self-directed learning as occurring when the learner

- Chooses to learn
- Consciously changes behavior, values, or knowledge
- Makes choices as to how to apply, what to read, what to do
- Is conscious of change and growth and can describe them
- Is free to speak, listen, interact, and consult
- Is free to challenge or question (Cranton, 1992, p. 55)

Self-directed learning is a goal, a process, and a learner characteristic that changes with the nature of the learning. Candy's framework of four distinct but interrelated phenomena (1991) may best capture and clarify the complexity of self-directed learning; I use this framework to discuss strategies for educator development.

Personal Autonomy

Drawing on the writing of several philosophers, Candy (1991, pp. 108–109) comes to the conclusion that an individual is seen to have personal autonomy to the extent that he or she

- Conceives of goals and plans independently of pressure from others
- Exercises freedom of choice in thought or action
- Uses the capacity for rational reflection to make judgments on the basis of morally defensible beliefs, as objectively as possible, and using relevant evidence
- Has the will and capacity to carry through plans of action arrived at through the process described above

- Exercises self-mastery in the face of reversals, challenges, and setbacks
- Has a concept of himself or herself as autonomous

Candy views this definition as an ideal, one which is not likely to be attained by the majority of individuals; not only are there many external threats to personal autonomy, but it is impossible to escape socializing influences on attitudes, values, and beliefs. Autonomy is also situation-specific, as are the other components of self-directed learning. A person can be more autonomous in career than in marriage, or more autonomous in learning about work-related topics than in learning new or abstract knowledge.

Educator Development and Personal Autonomy

As personal autonomy is viewed as both a goal and a process, I will maintain these two themes here. That is, one goal of development is to increase personal autonomy; a person works toward independence and freedom from constraints. Also, the process of development itself involves autonomous learning; a person grows and learns, in part, on his or her own. It is also important to note, however, that "autonomy should not be endorsed or promoted as a goal to the detriment of social interdependence" (Candy, 1991, p. 109).

Autonomy as a Goal

If educator development is to lead to autonomy, what might this mean for developmental strategies? In order to be autonomous, educators would need to

- Have the knowledge and skills to develop their own goals for professional development independently of any pressure
- Be free from inward or outward constraints or restrictions
- Be able to choose objectively from among alternatives based on their own beliefs and experiences
- Be able to develop a plan of action for development
- Be able to face reversals and challenges
- See themselves as autonomous

Clearly this is an ideal, for what educator would describe himself or herself as completely free from constraints, or being independent of any pressure from others? Most educators who work within institutions or organizations would not be able to achieve these goals. Perhaps this is why Mezirow (1985) writes, "There is probably no such thing as a self-directed learner" (p. 27). Yet, as goals, these aspects of personal autonomy are completely congruent with Mezirow's notion of transformative learning: "transformation can lead developmentally toward a more inclusive, differentiated, permeable, and integrated perspective" (1991, p. 155).

What can educators do to work toward personal and professional autonomy? Some aspects of developing autonomy can be individual projects, but others are enhanced by working with others. Candy (1991, p. 119) suggests that still other aspects of autonomy, such as "emotional autonomy or perseverance, are partly innate or, in any case, are rooted deeply in people's very earliest experiences at home and school." It is also clear that engagement in autonomous activities does not necessarily lead to personal or professional autonomy for all individuals. Similarly, no person can "make" another person autonomous; it is an individual goal.

Some strategies that have the potential to lead educators to the goals of personal autonomy are

- Developing the knowledge and skills for goal setting by reading thought-provoking books and articles
- Talking to experts, attending conferences, or otherwise gaining knowledge about educational practice through discussions with others
- Considering all the things that are seen to be outward constraints or restrictions (such as organizational policies, lack of resources, or shortages of money), and questioning the extent to which they are actually constraining practice
- Working with a trusted friend or colleague to discuss and question perceived inward constraints and restrictions—for example, insecurities, anxieties, fear of failure
- Listing all possible alternative approaches to practice (for example, different ways to structure a group, resources from the media, a change in physical location) based on one's own knowledge, beliefs, and experiences

- Choosing, from the listed alternatives, some approaches to try in practice and discussing the outcomes with a friend or colleague
- Developing a personal professional development plan based on the strategies already listed
- Preparing for reversals and challenges through self-reflection (perhaps keeping a journal) or through the development of a support network of colleagues
- Thinking of oneself as autonomous in practice while remembering that this does not imply solitude or indifference to the opinions of others

Autonomy as a Process

Educator development, when it leads to transformative or emancipatory learning, is an autonomous learning process. In other words, no other person can "teach" someone self-awareness, although another person can challenge, question, support, and otherwise foster the process. But because transformative learning involves changing underlying assumptions, beliefs, and values, it must essentially be directed by the self. It is a developmental process.

Drawing on the work of Piaget and others, Candy (1991, p. 118) summarizes the characteristics of heteronomy and autonomy. The features of heteronomy include egocentrism, unilateral respect, conformity, rigidity, blind faith in authority, other- directedness, and dependence. The characteristics of autonomy, on the other hand, include:

- Cooperation
- Mutual respect
- Individual creativity
- Flexibility
- Rational criticism
- Inner-directedness
- Independence

We can take this list and use it to describe educator development as an autonomous process. In such a developmental process, educators would

- Work cooperatively and collaboratively to learn more about their practice
- Respect the expertise of their colleagues and others working in educational development
- Be respected by their colleagues and others
- Be creative in their approach to their practice
- Be flexible and open to change in their practice
- Critically question their own practice and the practice of others
- Be open to critical questioning of their practice by others
- Possess an inner drive to develop their practice
- Work independently, without pressure from others, on the development of their practice

We would all probably like to see ourselves learning in this way, but it is one thing to list these ideals and quite another to engage in a learning process that has such characteristics. Some strategies that might foster this process are

- Organizing a professional discussion group in which ideas about practice are exchanged
- Setting up a list of peers and others who have particular expertise in one or more aspects of practice, and consulting those individuals as needed
- Sharing one's own knowledge, skills, and beliefs about practice
- Trying new strategies in one's practice, and being open about this with learners
- Changing and experimenting with one's practice based on discussions with learners and peers
- Questioning and reflecting on one's practice after each session, perhaps with the help of a journal or log
- Requesting comments from others, learners and peers, on one's practice
- Developing a personal vision of what practice would be like in an ideal state (without constraints) and deliberately working toward that vision
- Setting up a development plan independently of any other person's request or expectation

Educator Development and Personal Autonomy: An Illustration

Jo Anne is a trainer for a medium-sized industrial company. Her main responsibility is disseminating information about safety, new government regulations, and technological upgrading. Jo Anne has always been very interested in improving her practice and has been frustrated by the seeming lack of understanding demonstrated by the workers who are her learners. She sees herself as responsible when someone reports a violation of the safety procedures. Jo Anne has always attended any workshop or conference for which she could get funding from her company. She subscribes to *Training and Development* from her personal funds.

Although Jo Anne felt that she learned something from each workshop she attended and from some of the journal articles, it never seemed quite the same in her workplace. Worse, she did not have anyone else with whom she could discuss these concerns. Her supervisor consistently told her she was doing "a great job" and not to worry so much.

Jo Anne finally took a big step. She called a nearby university and asked if there was anyone there who specialized in training. She was given a name, and made an appointment to speak with him. The meeting began with Jo Anne saying, "I wondered if you could help me to get my learners to learn more." After some discussion of her practice and considerable questioning about the problem, Jo Anne was given some references and the names of two other trainers in the area with whom she could discuss her practice. Jo Anne was somewhat disappointed; she had hoped that the expert would be able to give her some simple things to try.

When I last spoke with Jo Anne, she had become extremely enthusiastic about Stephen Brookfield's *The Skillful Teacher,* and she was meeting "once in a while" with a colleague from another company. The most striking thing about that conversation with Jo Anne was that she said, "I realize I have to do it on my own—I always thought someone else should be able to show me. This just feels better, even though I really don't know any more than I did, and that's still frustrating."

Self-Management

Self-management is defined as the willingness and capacity to conduct one's own education (Candy, 1991). As a goal, this means development of the competence to direct one's learning, whether it be inside or outside formal educational settings. As a process, self-management involves making one's own decisions about learning. The relationship between personal autonomy and self-management is clear: the autonomous learner would engage in self-management. But what are the competencies that give a person the capacity to make learning decisions?

A considerable amount of research has been conducted in an attempt to describe the characteristics of individuals who direct their own learning. This was a primary focus of adult education research throughout the late 1960s and the 1970s. For example, in 1967, Miller linked Maslow's hierarchy of needs (1954) with Lewin's force-field theory (1947), creating a model to predict the extent to which learners would choose to participate in educational activities. The model includes a combination of personal factors and social forces, as does an early model developed by Boshier (1973). Cross (1992) incorporated life events and transitions as well as environmental factors into her chain-of-response (COR) model. Researchers continue to struggle with this issue. Henry and Basile's results (1994) emphasize the importance of social and insti-tutional factors, rather than personal characteristics. Stalker (1993) presents data to indicate that more adult learning is other-directed than we believe. She concludes that researchers should consider the "concept of voluntary participation in terms of its complex and multi-dimensional elements" (p. 74).

Educator Development and Self-Management

When educator development is self-managed, individuals have the goal of developing the competence to direct their own development, and they make their own decisions about the nature of the learning.

Self-Management as a Goal

Based on a survey of twenty authors' research, Candy (1991, p. 130) summarized the competencies that people would ideally have in order to manage their learning. They would

- Be methodical and disciplined
- Be logical and analytical

- Be reflective and self-aware
- Demonstrate curiosity, openness, and motivation
- Be flexible
- Be interdependent and interpersonally competent
- Be persistent and responsible
- Be venturesome and creative
- Show confidence and have a positive self-concept
- Be independent and self-sufficient
- Have developed information-seeking and retrieval skills
- Have knowledge about, and skill at, learning generally
- Develop and use defensible criteria for evaluating learning

Candy (1991) discusses the criticisms of the research on which this list is based, including, as examples, class and gender bias and a neglect of situational characteristics. However, if we consider the list as presenting possible self-management goals, rather than as profiling a self-directed learner, individual educators can reject those items that are irrelevant or inappropriate for themselves personally, for their contexts, or in specific situations.

How can we become "methodical and disciplined"? Some strategies that educators could try in order to move toward the goal of self-management include

- Developing a time management system which gives priority to the professional development activities of interest—for example, time for reading, one evening a week for a course, time for reflection after each session
- Setting specific professional development goals and developing a plan to work toward them
- Using a logical problem-solving model to determine what professional development activities would be most meaningful in a given context
- Engaging in activities that promote reflection and awareness, such as keeping a journal, videotaping and reviewing sessions, or writing educator autobiographies
- Being curious about educational practice: questioning others, soliciting alternative viewpoints, or watching others teach
- Being willing to change strategies when one strategy does not appear to be leading to further development

- Trying new things and taking risks, especially risking the possibility of appearing foolish or being wrong
- Turning to others for their expertise and ideas, whether it be a long-term mentor relationship, a group of colleagues, or a one-time consultation with an individual
- Not giving up just because a strategy does not produce immediate results; becoming more self-directed can involve difficult changes
- Describing one's developmental goals and activities positively to others
- Seeing and describing oneself as a person interested in developing practice
- Developing independence and self-sufficiency by engaging in some professional activities on one's own
- Learning how to access the literature and other resources through journals, libraries, and computer networks
- Developing a comfortable system for assessing learning, whether it be through feedback from others or self-analysis of journals, videotapes, and teaching materials based on defensible criteria

Self-Management as a Process

When educator development is a self-managed process, individuals make their own decisions about what they need to learn, how they will learn it, and if and when learning is taking place. This process is based on Knowles's original conceptualization of self-directed learning (1975). As with the other facets of self-directed learning, self-management is simultaneously a process and a goal.

The educator who is engaging in self-managed professional development could be

- Diagnosing development needs, with or without the assistance of others
- Setting development goals independently of pressure from others, but perhaps with the help of others
- Selecting sources of help for learning: materials, individuals, consultants, courses, or programs
- Determining what is personally meaningful, apart from the reward systems of the institution or organization

- Choosing to give up independent learning temporarily in order to gain basic knowledge and skills in a more formal setting
- Continuously reviewing the progress made in the chosen professional development activities
- Honestly acknowledging weaknesses and shortcomings
- Changing tactics when the current strategy is not meeting needs
- Evaluating professional development progress based on personal criteria

Educator Development and Self-Management: An Illustration

Michael is a counselor who has a private practice. One part of his practice involves leading what he calls "educational groups" in which he introduces participants to the various aspects of dysfunctional family dynamics. Over ten sessions, he leads people through a variety of role plays, simulations, and small-group activities to help them question their perceptions of their past and present roles in the family context. Some participants have been involved in individual counseling; others go on to individual counseling after the educational group has finished. Michael has formal training as a counselor but has been concerned for some time that he does not know enough about being an educator.

A friend suggested that Michael take an M.Ed. degree, but Michael did not want to give up that much of his time. Stimulated by this discussion, he decided to carefully analyze what he actually wanted to learn and then determine the best way of gaining that knowledge. He used a series of questions that he had prepared to help his clients untangle personal problems and applied those questions to his perceived practice problem. He discussed the results of this exercise with a friend, asking the friend to question him critically on each learning need that he expressed.

Michael came to the conclusion that he had, at least initially, two goals: he wanted to learn how people learn, and especially how individuals differed in the way they learned; and he wanted to know how to teach or present cognitive information. He felt that once he got started, he might refine these goals or add others.

In order to work toward the first goal, Michael decided to take an educational psychology course entitled "The Psychology of

Human Learning." He applied for special-student status, since he was not interested in course credit. When considering the second goal, Michael felt that the context in which his group worked was so specific that a course or workshop on presentation skills might not be relevant. He arranged, instead, for the professional development consultant from the local college to come and watch his work with his group and discuss it with him after each session. In exchange, he offered to put on a workshop series on counseling skills for the faculty at the consultant's college.

Now midway through both of these activities, Michael reports that he is "learning a lot," but he sees his initial goals as too "naïve." He has been reading about learning styles and has noticed that learning styles seem to be related to psychological type, a construct that he uses in his counseling practice. He plans to expand his reading and has already selected his next course.

Michael's circular way of approaching self-management may be fairly typical (for example, see Baskett, 1991). The development of practice, too, cannot be viewed as a linear sequence of learning experiences.

Learner Control

Learner control can be described as a "mode of organizing instruction in formal settings" (Candy, 1991, p. 23). This dimension of self-directed learning is usually thought of as a continuum (Millar, Morphet, and Saddington, 1986; Renner, 1983) ranging from almost total teacher control to almost total learner control. On one end of the continuum, when the educator is in control, he or she plays an expert role and uses methods such as lectures and demonstrations; on the other end, when the learner is in control, the educator may become a resource person or facilitator (Cranton, 1992). This concept of a continuum of learner control was popular in the 1960s, primarily in association with work on programmed and individualized instruction. As programmed instruction was based on the theoretical foundation of behaviorism, the concept of learner control was discarded along with behaviorism by the end of the 1970s. As I explored in my doctoral dissertation two decades ago (Cranton, 1976), the term was also used in relation to computer-assisted instruction; it still continues to be associated with computer-based education (see Gay, 1986). Candy (1991, p. 10) is careful to note that he does not intend to use this "specialized meaning," but in fact the concept is quite similar to his learner-control dimension. Within an organized setting, the degree of learner control is defined by the degree to which participants make decisions about the learning process.

Brookfield (1993, p. 233) sees learner control as a political issue: "Who controls the decisions concerning the ways and directions in which adults learn is a political issue highlighting the distribution of educational and political power. Who has the final say in framing the range and type of decisions that are to be taken, and in establishing the pace and mechanisms for decision making, indicates where control really resides." It is through this perspective that learner control moves beyond a mechanistic decision-making process and into an emancipatory learning process.

Educator Development and Learner Control

When educators are involved in formal development activities such as workshops, courses, and retreats, to what extent are they in control of the decision making about the content, structure, and methods of learning? As was discussed in Chapter Two, traditional development strategies tend to pay lip service at best to self-directed learning. We have all witnessed, too many times, the workshop leader who asks at the outset of the session for participants' expectations or objectives, writes them on chart paper, goes on to her or his own agenda, and perhaps or perhaps not refers to the list again at the end of the session.

As with the other dimensions of self-directed learning, learner control can be viewed as both a goal and a process. The goal is for educators to be able to make decisions about their professional development within institutions and organizations; the process is that of participating in that decision making.

Learner Control as a Goal

There are two aspects to learner control as a goal: one is that educators gain control over their professional development in organizations that may not encourage this; the other is that educators gain the knowledge and skills for decision making. The latter competencies are similar to those required for personal autonomy and self-management.

When control over developmental activities is a goal, educators can consider the following strategies:

- Working toward personal autonomy and self-management, using some of the suggestions presented earlier in this chapter
- Inquiring in advance of registering in a workshop, course, or program as to the extent to which participants will have control over their own learning and selecting only those in which control is promised
- Making suggestions to the professional development person or office as to the kinds of activities that would be of interest
- Volunteering to assist with professional development planning
- Asking workshop and course leaders to "permit" participant decision making
- Conducting sessions for colleagues in which participants have control over decisions, so as to act as a model

Learner Control as a Process

In order for the educator to engage in learner-controlled development in a formal setting, that setting must obviously provide the opportunity for it to occur. Most workshops, courses, or programs for educator development are somewhere on the continuum between total learner control and total control by others. The extent to which the following characteristics are present in development sessions indicates the degree to which they are a learner-controlled process:

- Educators' learning interests and needs are explored in advance of planning, ideally through discussion or observation of practice rather than the traditional needs assessment survey.
- Participants in the session are responsible for setting goals or objectives based on individual and group learning interests.
- Goals or objectives are periodically reviewed by the participants and modified as appropriate.
- The sequence and pace of the activities are determined by the participants through ongoing dialogue and review.
- The learning strategies are selected by the group and include variation so as to conform to individuals' preferences.
- All individuals (including the leader or facilitator) have access to learning resources and materials.

- Participants reflect on, discuss, and evaluate their own learning and development.
- Participants reflect on, discuss, and evaluate the quality of the sessions.

Educator Development and Learner Control: An Illustration

Vimla is a doctoral student specializing in medical education. She grew up in India and completed her undergraduate degree there. She describes that program as completely teacher-directed. During studies toward her master's degree, Vimla was careful to choose courses that were known for their rigor, heavy workload, and structure. She saw herself as a high-achieving student with high standards.

In the doctoral program, things became somewhat confusing for Vimla. There was one formal ongoing course, simply called the "Ph.D. seminar," in which students chose the topics to be investigated and led sessions. Some faculty usually attended, but there was no one teacher. Doctoral students could take any other courses they chose, but none were required. It was expected that students would read widely, complete comprehensive examinations, choose their research topic, and then register for the thesis. With the exception of some university requirements, the program was learner-controlled.

Vimla felt frustrated, helpless, and inadequate. Her usual reward system for learning was gone. She did not know how to make decisions about her own learning; she had never done so. Vimla's faculty adviser suggested that she treat the whole thing as an assignment with the objective of learning how to control learning. It is not an easy path for Vimla. She feels that much of her development is "superficial," and she continually seeks others' approval of her decisions. However, Vimla sees the importance of being able to control her own learning, especially in terms of her career development.

Autodidaxy

If I decide to learn about organic gardening because the Tennessee grub worm continues to mow down my tomato plants, I might buy books or go to the library, consult with my neighbors, experiment with various organic remedies, take notes on their effect, buy more tomato plants, and try again. This would be an example of autodidactic learning. Candy (1991) defines autodidaxy as intentional self-education. He writes: "It appears that adults learn how to build, how to buy, and how to borrow; they learn about languages and lampshades; about cooking and camping; about making wine; about music, art, literature, history, science, and psychology. In short, no domain of human existence or inquiry is exempt from the self-educational efforts of these avid amateurs, whose serious self-set study often eclipses both the breadth and intensity of even the best-informed practitioners and scholars" (Candy, 1991, p. 159).

It was in Tough's (1979) well-known study on individual learning projects that autodidaxy was first operationalized and investigated. Despite the criticisms leveled against Tough's work, he did establish that a large proportion of adults engage in sustained and independent learning pursuits. He also sparked considerable interest in the research community; numerous studies were conducted in a variety of settings and with different subgroups of the population to replicate and refine Tough's investigation. Candy (1991, p. 159) concludes that "80 to 100 percent of the adult population" may engage in autodidactic learning, and that it "is not confined to any particular social, educational, occupational, or ethnic categories, but is widespread—almost universal—among adults."

Educator Development and Autodidaxy

Autodidaxy may be an ideal form of learning. One can see that if all constraints are removed and individuals have control, free will, and access to resources, autodidactic learning will be the natural ideal. Jarvis (1992b, p. 133) comments that in autodidactic learning, individuals "are responsible to themselves alone." Professional educators are individuals who would seem to be more likely to engage in autodidaxy than other subgroups (for example, see Addleton, 1984).

The goal-versus-process distinction may not be as clear in this facet of self-directed learning as it is in the other three facets. Working toward autodidactic learning as a goal means that the individual will also be engaged in independent learning. When autodidaxy is a goal of educators' development, they will strive to become independent of formal or organized developmental activities. As a process, autodidactic learning involves educators' initiating and carrying out their own development projects.

Autodidaxy as a Goal

What should the educator who wants to pursue independent learning projects do? Tough (1979) treated this question as an organizational one: selecting a space and time for learning, obtaining resources, and setting deadlines. However, if a person has always relied on formal settings to provide opportunities for learning, these preparatory steps may not address the issue. Individual educators will have different preferences as to how to work toward autodidactic learning as a goal. Some of the following strategies may be helpful:

- Keeping a notebook of ideas of possible learning projects
- Collecting resources of any kind that are relevant to areas of interest, including making notes of people who have expertise in appropriate areas
- Conducting a self-analysis of one's practice: deciding what areas are of interest for further learning and what areas are already strengths
- Obtaining any prerequisite knowledge through taking instruction in a formal setting
- Experimenting with small learning projects, perhaps projects unrelated to professional practice
- Writing a description of what are usually the obstacles or blocks to independent learning, and reflecting on the validity of this description
- Asking colleagues and friends about their independent learning projects and how they conducted them
- Writing about or describing oneself verbally as a learner, and having a colleague or friend ask critical questions
- Listing and experimenting with ways to conduct a learning project differently from how one usually learns

Autodidaxy as a Process

Researchers who have attempted to describe the process of autodidactic learning have looked for organized patterns of steps that people go through. Candy (1991) is critical of this approach, pointing out that respondents try to please the researcher in their answers, that they may report socially acceptable learning methods rather than those they use, and that they may not be conscious of how they engage in learning projects. Individual differences among educators as learners are probably greater than the regularities. For some, learning projects may resemble problem-solving processes; for others, their intuition might lead the way. Some educators will look for collaborative projects; others will prefer to work alone. I have argued elsewhere (Cranton, 1994a) that psychological type preference (Jung, [1921] 1971) may provide an explanation for the different processes individuals go through in their learning. (See Chapter Six for a detailed discussion of this topic.) In addition, the content and context of the learning will influence the process (see Danis and Tremblay, 1987).

Some strategies that educators can consider using in an autodidactic learning process are

- Developing a systematic action plan that includes objectives, resources, and methods of learning
- Finding a learning partner, a mentor, or a group of colleagues who are interested in the same topic
- Designing a practical experience or set of experiences from which to learn (for example, volunteering to work on a curriculum committee in order to learn about curriculum development)
- Exploring all possible learning strategies and letting intuition guide one through
- Setting aside a quiet time alone for reading, reflecting, and writing
- Asking for ongoing feedback from others (students, colleagues, a professional developer) to guide the process

Educator Development and Autodidaxy: An Illustration

Edgar describes himself as an environmentalist, an activist, and an enthusiastic member of the green movement—"No capitals," he usually adds, to separate himself from the Green Party. It is unclear to Edgar's acquaintances what he actually does, for he always seems to be running from one meeting or conference to another, rather than "working." Edgar involves himself in working with community groups, organizing campaigns against projects that he sees as detrimental to the environment, publishing a newsletter, and writing on a wide variety of issues of interest to him.

Edgar has a background in education. He once was an elementary school teacher but resigned when he found the system oppressive. He decided that his experience in working with children was not adequate to help him best work with his community groups. Edgar's view of formal educational institutions was not conducive to leading him to register in a course on adult education, so he decided to begin an exploratory independent learning project.

In his intuitive way, Edgar ferreted out all discussion groups in the region that bore any resemblance to adult education; he collected numerous books, articles, and reports on education and the philosophy of education; and he began simultaneously to meet adult educators, talk about adult education, and read the literature. He had no systematic plan and could not articulate goals aside from the general one of learning about adult education. Edgar never missed a discussion group. He enjoyed describing his work with community groups and asking others for comments on his practice. He circulated drafts of articles for feedback. In no way observable to another person, Edgar must have decided that he had reached his goal; the last time I saw him, he was involved in another set of discussion groups on a different topic.

Summary

In order for educators to engage in transformative developmental activities, self-directed learning needs to be a component of the process. Explicating one's assumptions about practice, questioning those assumptions, and possibly revising them can only be conducted by the educator himself or herself. This is not to say, of course, that professional development is a solitary activity or is not stimulated by direction from others, but rather that the process is finally directed and controlled by the individual.

After a brief look at the history of self-directed learning, I have adopted Candy's framework of four distinct but interrelated phenomena (1991) in order to discuss educator development. Self-direction is seen to have the dimensions of personal autonomy, self-management, learner control, and autodidaxy. Each dimension is both a goal and a process.

In order to foster personal autonomy in their development, educators work toward freeing themselves from constraints, both personal and institutional, but they work cooperatively and collaboratively with others. Self-management involves the development of competence to make one's own decisions about learning. When working in formal settings, educators may have some degree of control over the decisions made; learner control is another dimension of self-directedness that can be developed. Finally, educators pursue independent learning projects related to their practice and thus engage in autodidactic learning. For each of these dimensions, an illustrative case study has been presented.

Chapter Four

Critical Reflection

I always enjoyed teaching research methods and statistics. It provided a contrast with my university work in adult education and instructional development and called on my old expertise from my graduate studies. I often gave workshops for people outside of the higher education context—trainers, government departments, health councils—and enjoyed the "expert" role. But I never reflected very much on what I did.

Then, when I was invited to give a four-day workshop series on research methods that included the quantitative, qualitative, and critical research paradigms, I encountered a discrepancy in my thinking about the processes I used in my adult education seminars and my research workshops. This led me to reexamine my approaches in both areas and, over some time, to a shift in perspective in both areas. In retrospect, it seems simple; at the time, I felt that my insights were critical to my philosophy of practice.

Critical reflection is the central process in transformative learning. Our natural human interest in emancipation drives us to reflect on the way we see ourselves, our history, our knowledge, and our social roles. If we see that we are constrained or oppressed by any of our perspectives, we may be challenged to revise them. And so human beings learn, change, and develop. Following Habermas (1971), Mezirow writes, "Emancipatory knowledge is knowledge gained through critical self-reflection, as distinct from the knowledge gained from our 'technical' interest in the objective world or our 'practical' interest in social relationships. The form of inquiry in critical self-reflection is appraisive rather than prescriptive or designative" (Mezirow, 1991, p. 87).

Although critical reflection is emphasized in most educational contexts (for example, in teacher education) and often described as a goal of education, there are surprisingly few references to reflection by adult learning theorists. Meyers (1986) writes about critical thinking in higher education; Brookfield (1987) has popularized the term in the adult education literature. Dirkx (1989) writes about reflection in education in the professions as well as some broader conceptualizations of learning from experience. Yet in a review of adult learning theory, Merriam and Caffarella (1991) have only one reference to critical reflection, and that reference is contained within a description of transformative learning theory. Similarly, in Merriam's update on adult learning theory (1993), the only reference to reflection is to Mezirow's work (Clark, 1993).

If educators are to develop their practice, a process including both personal and professional growth, then critical reflection on practice will be central to the learning. This is not to say that instrumental and communicative learning about teaching are not a part of becoming an educator, but rather that *development* requires moving beyond the acquisition of new knowledge and understanding, into questioning our existing assumptions, values, and perspectives.

In this chapter, I first briefly review some definitions of and approaches to critical reflection. Mezirow's differentiation between content, process, and premise reflection (1991) will be discussed, as this is a key concept in transformative learning. I will then propose some strategies for educators who wish to engage in critical reflection on their practice. The strategies will be based, in part, on Brookfield's suggestions (1987) for developing critical thinking and in part on Mezirow's more theoretical conceptualization of critical self-reflection.

Defining Critical Reflection

Most educators quote Dewey (1933) in a discussion of reflection. He defined reflection as "active, persistent and careful consideration of any belief or supposed form of knowledge in the light of the grounds that support it and the further conclusion to which it tends" (p. 9). Dewey wanted people to learn how to think, how to "discriminate between beliefs that rest upon tested evidence and those that do not" (p. 97). When people think, they delay action until they (1) understand the situation thoroughly, (2) know the goal they want to reach, (3) consider as many options as possible for reaching that goal, (4) weigh the options, and (5) make a plan, all before taking action.

Reflection as Problem Solving

Dewey's writing about reflection was in the context of thinking and problem solving. He considered being able to discriminate between those things that are beliefs and those things that are based on evidence to be "the central factor in all reflective or distinctly intellectual thinking" (1933, p. 11). This early discussion bears a close resemblance to Mezirow's interpretation of critical self-reflection (1991). With Boud, Keough, and Walker's addition (1985) of the affective domain (feelings and beliefs) to Dewey's definition, we have a view that is consistent with transformative learning theory.

Reflection as an Intuitive Process

An alternate and influential view of reflection is provided by Schön (1983). Unlike Dewey's description of reflection as a rational process, Schön sees it as largely unarticulated and intuitive. He writes

> When a practitioner reflects in and on his practice, the possible objects of his reflection are as varied as the kinds of phenomena before him and the systems of knowing-in-practice which he brings to them. He may reflect on the tacit norms and appreciations that underlie a judgment or on the strategies and theories implicit in a pattern of behavior. He may reflect on the feeling for a situation that has led him to adopt a particular course of action, on the way in which he has framed the problem he is trying to solve, or on the role he has constructed for himself within a larger institutional context (Schön, 1983, p. 62).

Schön's description rounds out the definition of reflection. He points out the limitations of technical rationality and attempts to explain how people "think on their feet" or "just know what to do." Not all individuals are rational and orderly in considering their practice; yet they do engage in reflection. Reflection could be, for different people, unarticulated intuitions, a detailed review of an experience, a logical analysis, or an evaluation of feelings.

Reflection and Interaction

Interaction with others is a vital component of transformative learning. Schön's notion of practitioners reflecting in the midst of action tends not to leave very much opportunity for discussion with others. Boud and his colleagues (Boud, Keough, and Walker, 1985; Boud and Walker, 1991, 1992) initially emphasized reflection after an experience but later incorporated reflection during action into their thinking. This conceptualization allows discussion with others to be a component of reflection. Brookfield's approach to developing critical reflection (1987) incorporates group activities and group discussion: others play a role in helping a person identify his or her assumptions, question the validity of assumptions, and so forth.

It is Jarvis (1992b) who best links reflection to working with others, as an educator does: "Significantly, in seeking to achieve another's development, individuals are themselves engaged in the highest forms of reflective learning, and they themselves grow and develop" (p. 115). Educators learn with their students; similarly, professional developers learn with educators. This is, of course, Freire's thesis (1970): that teachers and students learn together through dialogue.

Jarvis (1992b) also points out the paradox between reflective learning as the "highest form of learning" (p. 117) and society's curtailments of achieving this goal. He poses the question of whether society (a normative system) could exist if everyone tried to learn reflectively and to encourage the development of other people. This paradox is a fundamental concept in emancipatory knowledge: through emancipatory learning (and therefore critical self-reflection), we become aware of constraints of social systems and try to free ourselves from them.

Reflection as a Developmental Process

Another interrelated approach to reflection is to describe it as a developmental process. This, too, is congruent with Mezirow's view of transformative learning, which he sees as developmental. Drawing on the early work of Perry (1970) and others, King and Kitchener (1994) provide one such model, the Reflective Judgment Model. They describe seven stages in all.

The first three are prereflective stages, where individuals do not acknowledge or perhaps even see that knowledge is uncertain, and they therefore do not understand that there are problems for which there are no correct answers. The next two stages are termed quasi-reflective. In stage four, there is a recognition that knowledge is uncertain and knowledge claims are idiosyncratic, but no discriminations are made between the quality of individuals' opinions. In stage five, knowledge is seen as subjective because it is an individual's perception. There is a greater awareness of the validity of different perspectives based on evidence.

King and Kitchener (1994) describe only the last two stages of development as reflective thinking: "People who reason with the assumptions of these stages argue that knowledge is not a 'given' but must be actively constructed and that claims of knowledge must be understood in relation to the context in which they were generated. Furthermore, those reasoning with Stage 6 or 7 assumptions argue that while judgments must be grounded in relevant data, conclusions should remain open to reevaluation" (p. 66).

At the highest stage of this model, reflection is defined as a rational process: "Beliefs are justified on the basis of a variety of interpretive considerations, such as the weight of the evidence, the explanatory value of the interpretations, the risk of erroneous conclusions, consequences of alternative judgments, and the interrelationships of these factors. Conclusions are defended as representing the most complete, plausible, or compelling understanding of an issue on the basis of the available evidence" (King and Kitchener, 1994, p. 16). This rational approach mirrors Dewey's discussion of reflection (1933) and is similar to what we find generally in the literature where reflection is described as a developmental process.

Reflection in Transformative Learning

Critical reflection is the central process in transformative learning. Clearly, not all critical reflection leads to transformation; we can question things without changing them. To be transformative, reflection has to involve and lead to some fundamental change in perspective. But transformative learning takes place through reflection, in one form or another (see Chapters Five and Seven).

As we have just seen, King and Kitchener (1994) speak of "reflective judgement" as logical reasoning. Brookfield (1987) nicely links critical thinking (he uses the term critical thinking to mean the same as Mezirow's critical reflection) with emancipatory learning: "One alternative interpretation of the concept of critical thinking is that of *emancipatory learning*" (p. 12). He also is clear in saying that "[b]eing a critical thinker involves more than cognitive activities such as logical reasoning or scrutinizing arguments for assertions unsupported by empirical evidence. Thinking critically involves our recognizing the assumptions underlying our beliefs and behaviors" (p. 13). He describes critical thinking as involving "a reflective dimension" (p. 14).

Although Jarvis is critical of Brookfield for including creativity as a part of critical thinking, calling this "rather illogical" (Jarvis, 1992b, p. 113), it seems that critical reflection is a broader process than that of technical rationality (Schön, 1983). Brookfield suggests that the components of critical thinking are identifying and challenging assumptions, exploring and imagining alternatives, and analysis and action. In this chapter, I use these components, along with Mezirow's description, to suggest strategies for educators to engage in critical reflection on their practice.

Recently, Brookfield (1994) again broadened his conception of critical reflection. He defines it as consisting of "two interrelated processes: (1) learning to question, and then to replace or reframe, an assumption that is accepted by majority opinion as representing common sense, and, (2) taking a perspective on social and political structures, or on personal and collective actions, that is strongly alternative to that held by the majority" (p. 55). Although his earlier definitions clearly have an implied political facet, it is explicitly and strongly stated here. With this approach, reflection has become far removed from the problem-solving approach of Dewey or even from the common usage of the word, which is rather more akin to introspection.

Brookfield (1994) also describes five themes that he found in educators' reports of critical reflection: impostership, the sense that critical reflection is not appropriate for that person; cultural suicide, the realization that others may not approve of the changes or potential changes; lost innocence, acknowledging ambiguities and dilemmas; roadrunning, the recognition of a process that has states of limbo, like being suspended in midair; and the importance of community or support from others. These themes were observed in the writing or dialogue of 337 educators over eleven years. In this conceptualization, critical reflection clearly has the potential to lead to transformation; solving problems about one's practice would not lead to thoughts of cultural suicide.

Three Types of Reflection

Mezirow (1991) distinguishes among *content, process,* and *premise reflection,* a distinction useful in both clarifying the definition of reflection and understanding transformative learning.

Content Reflection

Individuals may reflect on the content or description of a problem. For example, if the problem seems to be one of student motivation, the educator might look for indicators of high or low motivation and attempt to associate those student behaviors with his or her own teaching strategies. If the educator then notices that students seem to be more motivated when visual aids are used, humor is expressed, and when group work is incorporated into the session, an experiment might be conducted in which these strategies are used more frequently and student behavior is again observed. Content reflection is similar to Dewey's definition of reflection, referred to earlier in this chapter.

Process Reflection

Process reflection involves thinking about the strategies used to solve the problem rather than the content of the problem itself. The educator interested in student motivation might ask whether or not the effort to find indicators of motivation was adequate. Were the indicators relevant? Were they dependable? If the same problem came up in another class, would the same procedure solve the problem? This is still a rational and orderly kind of reflection and does not incorporate Schön's intuitive component (1983) even though Mezirow says it is also "the way we learn in metaphorical-abductive problem solving" (1991, p. 105). However, process reflection would be a part of Brookfield's approach to critical thinking (1987).

Premise Reflection

Premise reflection leads us to question the relevance of the problem itself. The educator might ask, "Is student motivation my concern or responsibility?" "Can teachers motivate students at all?" "Is motivation a valid concept?" In premise reflection, the assumptions, beliefs, or values underlying the problem are questioned. Distinct from problem solving, this process can lead to transformative learning.

Strategies for Critical Reflection in Educator Development

Educators may accept their practice as it is, "tinkering" with some aspects of their performance, the organization of the content, or the activities they use. They may engage in reflection-in-action, as described by Schön (1983), intuitively reacting to the complex nuances of the interactions among learners. Educators may also work to describe, question, and develop their philosophy of practice; it is here, I believe, that there is the most potential for meaningful growth.

I now turn to strategies that educators can use to engage in critical reflection on their practice. It should be noted again that critical reflection does not necessarily lead to transformative learning, but it is an essential component. The strategies suggested in this chapter may foster critical reflection but not lead to changed perspectives on practice. Chapter Five focuses on transformative learning.

Articulating Assumptions

The assumptions that we make in order to interpret the world around us are deeply ingrained, taken for granted, and difficult to articulate. A part of the definition of the word assumption is "taken for granted," meaning that we are unlikely to be aware of holding this supposition. Unless a person has developed good critical-reflection skills and has hurtled off the cliff into midair many times (as with Wile E. Coyote, to use Brookfield's 1994 Roadrunner analogy), it is probably not possible to articulate assumptions without the help of others. This need not take place in a formal consultation or in a group, but some discussion with others facilitates seeing what assumptions we make.

Assumptions made by educators about their practice can be the product of their experiences as learners, the values held by their family or in their community, the knowledge that they have gained about teaching and learning, and their experiences as educators, among dozens of other possibilities. If simply asked to list or talk about the assumptions underlying their practice, most people could not do that. Yet, in order to engage in practice that is guided by a well-thought-out philosophy, and in order to change and develop as an educator, it is important to make these assumptions explicit.

Several techniques for making assumptions explicit are suggested in the literature, in the context of educators helping learners engage in critical reflection. Brookfield (1987) suggests critical questioning (to be discussed in a later section of this chapter), critical-incident exercises, criteria analysis, role play and critical debate, and crisis-decision simulations as ways to help others examine their assumptions. What these techniques have in common is that they require individuals to think about specific situations, whether they be real or imagined, and then to examine how decisions are or would be made in those situations. This, in turn, helps a person to see what assumptions underlie those decisions. If, for example, in a crisis-decision simulation (an activity where people imagine a situation in which they must make a choice from among a number of uncomfortable options), I choose to save the teacher rather than the pregnant mother from certain death, this will tell me something about my assumptions about education. Similarly, if I describe, as a critical incident, a high point in my practice—say, a time when learners challenged my right to control the agenda of a session—an assumption about my philosophy of practice underlies the choice of this incident.

Educators who attend workshops, conferences, or courses in adult education will likely encounter strategies such as these, whether or not they are explicitly used to help them examine assumptions about practice. Brookfield (1987) adds that "[f]riends, spouses, lovers, colleagues, and support group members can prompt us to become aware of our hidden assumptions" (p. 110).

Apart from participation in activities specifically designed to promote increased awareness of assumptions, what can educators do to explicate the assumptions underlying their practice? Here are some suggestions:

- Keep a shared journal with a trusted friend or colleague in which both people write about their practice and exchange the journal, looking for assumptions in each other's writing.
- Write a biography of oneself as an educator and discuss it with another person in order to find hidden assumptions.
- Choose a person one knows who has a quite different philosophy of practice, and attempt to write a philosophy of practice from that person's perspective, analyzing it for assumptions and contrasting it with one's own perspective.
- Write a description of one's philosophy of practice and justify it to a colleague or friend.
- Analyze videotapes of one's practice and justify behavior to oneself or to another person.
- Discuss one's philosophy of practice with learners, asking them to challenge and question what is said.
- Find a colleague who seems to share one's philosophy of practice, and hold a mutual hunt for assumptions.
- Write a description of the philosophy of practice of one's favorite educator from the past and analyze the assumptions underlying that philosophy.

Determining Sources and Consequences of Assumptions

Knowing where in our history our assumptions came from and understanding the consequences of holding those assumptions is a vital component of self-awareness and therefore of critical reflection. Mezirow (1990) writes: "Perhaps the most significant kind of adult learning involves bringing psychocultural assumptions into critical consciousness to help learners understand how they have come into possession of conceptual categories, rules, tactics, and criteria for judging that are implicit in their habits of perception, thought and behavior. Such transformative learning enhances our crucial sense of agency over ourselves and our lives" (p. 361). When we understand what we believe and its roots (whether those be in our childhood, our past experiences, our culture, our language, or the media), then we become free to choose whether or not we want to maintain that belief. Without knowing the source of our assumptions, it is difficult to feel free to question them.

Understanding the consequences of having certain expectations is equally important in becoming free to choose. If a person believes that it is the responsibility of the government to ensure that everyone becomes literate, a consequence of that belief could be that the person makes no effort to help others learn. Being unaware of the consequence leaves a person constrained in his or her choices.

Quite often when we uncover assumptions, we also realize where they came from. A person will say, "I can't believe I said that; that's what my mother used to say," or "That's the way we were treated when I was in the university." The source of the assumption becomes clear, along with the understanding that this is a current expectation of how things are in the world.

The consequences of holding certain assumptions may not be as readily available to us. For example, people will say, "That's just the way things go" when talking about the outcomes of a situation or even the outcomes of their own behavior. However, critical questioning, discussion, and practice will lead to the development of insights into consequences.

In workshops, courses, seminars, or any development session organized by others, educators may encounter learning activities such as role plays, critical incidents, or repertory grids. As mentioned earlier, such activities can be very useful in making assumptions explicit. However, they do not necessarily help us understand the sources and consequences of assumptions unless a special effort is made to incorporate this into the activity.

Individual activities such as keeping a journal, writing a life story, and writing or telling an educational autobiography are useful for articulating assumptions as well as focusing attention on their sources and consequences. Working alone, with a partner, or in a small group, educators can ask questions of themselves and each other to facilitate this process:

- Was there a time when I did not hold this belief?
- Can I remember when I first believed this?
- Was there an influential person in my life who held this belief?
- Was this belief prevalent in my family, my community, or my past educational contexts?
- Is this a commonly held belief in the organization or institution in which I work?
- Do I associate any special incident with this belief?
- If I did not believe this, how would I act differently?
- If I continue to believe this, how will I act?
- Do these actions feel right for me?
- What other people are affected by my believing this?

Critical Questioning

When people are clear about what their assumptions are and where they came from, they then have the choice of questioning those assumptions. Assumptions that have been uncritically assimilated from past experiences or current contexts can be assessed for their validity.

Mezirow (1991) argues that this validation process almost always involves rational discourse "[b]ecause validity testing of contested meaning is so central to understanding the conditions under which the meaning of a communicated idea is true and because so much of what we need to understand must be consensually validated" (1991, p. 77). Just as discourse is central to questioning our beliefs and assumptions, so does engaging in discourse lead us to "more developmentally advanced meaning perspectives" (Mezirow, 1991, p. 78). Participation in rational discourse requires that one can question, be questioned, and assess arguments. Similarly, among its other features, a more developmentally advanced meaning perspective is objective and rational in assessing arguments, critically reflective of presuppositions, and able to accept consensus for judging validity claims. In other words, to grow, one has to question; when one grows, one is better able to question. It is easier for most people to do this with the help of others.

Brookfield (1987) describes critical questioning as an effective means for externalizing ingrained assumptions; however, it is an equally important means for examining the validity of assumptions that have been articulated. Brookfield suggests that very few people naturally possess the skills of good critical questioning, and he provides guidelines for developing those skills: be specific; relate the questions to particular events, people, and actions; work from the particular to the general; and be conversational. Critical questioning is not just asking questions. It is working to get underneath the assumptions we hold and sorting out whether or not they hold up under scrutiny. It is difficult to ask such questions of both ourselves and others in an open, authentic, and nonthreatening way.

. The nature and content of critical questioning will vary with the assumptions being questioned. In order to illustrate this, I use two examples from my practice, with permission from the educators involved.

Carole teaches Health Care Aide and Nursing Theory in a continuing education program associated with a secondary school. She has a new and tentative belief in self-directed learning as a goal of education; she also has several still-unquestioned but articulated assumptions about her practice. I give excerpts from a letter she wrote to me, followed by questions that could be posed for her consideration. Carole wrote:

> Help! Enclosed please find an outline of insanity gone berserk! I instituted some SDL projects in my Nursing Theory only to find that upon testing—their choice—they either completely failed or did miserably. I'm now looking up your SDL model to see where I went wrong. They were so enthused, hungry, co-operative. I taught the rest of the class, I thought, so well. The test was easy, using only knowledge and comprehension level questions. What am I missing? Their success was the one constant I have depended on!

If, as developers, we were working with Carole, what might we ask? We could, in conversation, or in a written response to her letter, question her assumptions about the concept of self-directed learning.

• You instituted self-directed learning projects; is the assumption here that this is your responsibility alone? Why do you believe that? Do you see a contradiction between the concept of self-directed learning and how you have implemented it?

What does this lead to in terms of your students' perceptions of "SDL projects"?

Carole also seems to be making assumptions about testing and where the responsibility for testing lies. It might be helpful if we discussed these, including some of the following questions in our conversation:

- They chose to be tested. You have accepted an espoused assumption about self-directed learning. What are the results of accepting this assumption? Are you saying that you would implement whatever strategy the students asked for? What if they asked not to be self-directed?
- You designed the test. Is the assumption here that this is your job? Why? What effect might this have on students' perceptions of your role and their roles? Would it work to have students involved in designing an evaluation?
- Do you see yourself as responsible for their poor performance on your test? Why do you believe this? What does it lead to? What are students responsible for?
- Why did you prepare what you describe as an "easy" test? Does this mean that you really did not believe they would have learned very much? That you wanted to ensure their success? What was this decision based on? Why might it have led to poor results?

If critical questions are a part of a conversation, or written in the margins of a journal, along with other kinds of comments, they will be thought-provoking and challenging. When educators work together to critically question their assumptions about their practice, or when a professional developer works with an educator, care must be taken not to question in an intimidating or threatening way. Even asking "Why do you believe that?" can be an intimidating question if it is not set in a reflective and caring context.

My second example is from an educational autobiography written by an educator who works in a college library (used with her permission). Sue has taught once in a classroom setting, just recently, but she is involved in working individually with students every day in the library. The autobiography was written as one strategy for uncovering underlying assumptions about Sue's practice. It starts when she was five years old and describes educational experiences up to the present (Sue may be in her mid- to late thirties). The writing is in the third person for the first two-thirds of the story but then changes to the first person. I will provide some quotations in which assumptions are being articulated and then suggest critical questions that could be asked.

Sue wrote:

> School, however, held no particular interest for Susan, other than the opportunity to socialize. This often caused problems for her. . . . This was in strict contrast to the way she behaved at home, where she was fairly quiet and well behaved, extremely shy around adults. [introvert at home; extravert at school?]

> For the first time, Sue took education seriously. It was important to her to succeed. She was intent on being as independent as possible. If she did not succeed, she was only answerable to herself. [underlying assumption: if I fail I am responsible, and only I have the right to judge?]

> Sue really enjoyed her job, often describing it as an opportunity to learn something new every day. She was actively "teaching" library skills to classes of students visiting the library. . . .

> In fact, the implicit theory which was revealed for Sue through reflection was around the issue of self-esteem in the academic arena. [this last term "arena" seems to me to be a metaphor—is there possibly an underlying assumption that I think of academic life as an area where one must "perform" or be eaten by lions?]

> I never learned how to be a student, therefore I *assume* that this is the reason I do not have much faith in my ability to be a good student now. This past summer I identified strongly with the "imposter syndrome."

There are many possible responses to Sue's journal, of course. We could include some of the following critical questions:

• There seems to be a contradiction between enjoying something and learning something, at least learning in a formal setting. Why is this an issue for you? Are you saying that learning is not enjoyable for you? What are the consequences of believing this?

- Why was independence so important? This surfaced when you became a college student. Was there something that precipitated this? How did this goal change your behavior? Is learning independently more valuable than learning collaboratively?
- Learning on the job is enjoyable for you, but not learning in an institutional setting. What is the difference? Where does your perception of formal learning come from? Has this perception shaped your perception of yourself as an educator?
- Your confidence and self-esteem as a learner in the university seems to be low. Was this always the case? Is this related to the "bad" reports you received in school as a child? (The relevant quote for this piece has not been included here.) Can you reconcile this perception with your educational achievements?
- You assume that a person needs to learn how to be a student. What does this mean? Why do you believe this? How has this influenced your perception of yourself as an educator?

As in Carole's case, the questioning between individuals has to be sensitive and caring. Sue revealed in her story many personal incidents from her childhood; her openness must be treated gently. Yet Sue confirmed that interaction with others was needed. At the end of her autobiography, she wrote that she had tried to identify underlying assumptions but did not feel that she was very successful. She felt she needed to discuss the story.

Imagining Alternatives

In transformative learning theory (to be discussed in Chapter Five), not very much has been written about how assumptions or perspectives get revised. It is usually just the stage that follows a questioning of the validity of underlying assumptions. It is likely that different people go about this process in different ways (as will be discussed in Chapter Six), but being able to see alternatives to one's invalidated assumptions is, in some form, a component of critical reflection.

In his discussion of critical thinking, Brookfield (1987) describes techniques for imagining alternatives within the larger framework of developing alternative ways of thinking. As he points out, imagining alternatives requires that people "break with existing patterns of thought and action" (Brookfield, 1987, p. 117), something easier said than done. But that is one of the characteristics of critical reflection that makes it a central process in transformative learning.

Some of Brookfield's suggestions (1987) for imagining alternatives are summarized here.

- Brainstorming is a group activity during which participants generate as many different ideas as possible, without judgment of the quality of the ideas. There is a tendency for the unusual nature of the suggestions to increase as people become comfortable with the process and realize the enjoyment. Ideas are said to piggyback on each other, that is, one idea from one person suggests a related idea from another person.
- Preferred scenarios are descriptions of how things would be ideally. Working with someone, people consider questions such as "What would this problem look like if it were managed better?" and "What would exist that does not exist now?" The educator could consider what his or her ideal practice scenario would be like: "If I had a perfect group of learners or a perfect class, what would it be like?"
- A futures invention process is one in which participants go through questioning who they are, what they want to do, how they can do it, and which other people will join in making the inventions. Intended to be held as a retreat or residential workshop, people go through a structured set of nine exercises, leading to an imagined future. However, individuals or small groups could set up a similar, less-structured process in which they designed, planned, or imagined what their future could be.
- Immersion in an aesthetic or artistic experience can lead to imagining alternatives, especially for people who normally think in linear problem-solving ways. Brookfield (1987) suggests writing poetry, creating fantasies, drawing, photography, songwriting, and dramatizing problems or situations as some media for stimulating imagination of alternatives.

Other strategies that educators might consider in order to see their world in different ways could be

- Visualization exercises, in which one creates scenarios in the mind's eye and allows oneself to "go with" the scene as it unfolds
- Consulting with imaginative friends or colleagues and enlisting their help in imagining alternatives
- Turning the process into an exercise conducted with one's learners (saying "Here is my dilemma; what alternatives can you see?" and forming groups or teams to generate ideas)
- Reading about approaches or perspectives that one has never before considered feasible or practical, and trying to remain open to the ideas presented
- Changing roles with a friend or colleague who has a different perspective and arguing from each other's point of view

Being able to imagine alternatives is closely linked with a person's learning style, personality, or psychological type, as will be discussed in Chapter Six. This may be one of the most difficult components of critical reflection for those individuals who do not easily see alternatives. De Bono's (1971) attempts to develop a systematic procedure for thinking in different ways provide one illustration of this difficulty; most nonintuitive types experience frustration at trying to complete the activities, and intuitive or imaginative people do not see the need for the book. The command "Imagine alternative ways of seeing your practice" does not work. Yet this key component of critical reflection has to be there if people are to develop.

An illustration may help. When Patti was a university student, in her formative years as an educator, behaviorism and the scientific method were the popular perspectives. She learned about the importance of being objective and scientific. She understood learning in terms of human response to stimuli. This appealed to Patti's way of thinking, and she whole-heartedly accepted this view of the world. She was challenged by friends and colleagues but saw the world so clearly that no challenge was taken seriously. Twenty years later almost everyone around Patti was talking a different language. They were reading qualitative research studies, seeing learning as a complex phenomenon, talking about the collective unconscious, expressing enthusiasm about using archetypes in understanding learning.

Patti was led to question her assumptions about her practice, quite painfully. But she was not good at imagining alternatives. She often said, "I don't get it—I don't know how to replace my old ideas, yet I know they're wrong." She talked to others but remained skeptical of their responses.

It was finally a comprehensive reading program that led Patti to feel free to develop her perspective on her practice. This she did alone and almost without discussion with others. She read what she called "the most weird things," many of which were rejected but some of which were used to form a new view. In the end, one book led her to a new, comfortable, integrated view. But as she described it, "I was ready; that book just pushed me off the edge."

Summary

It is through critical reflection on their practice that educators come to see their expectations of themselves, their learners, and the larger place of education in our society. The reflective educator can then examine these assumptions and become free to choose to revise them if they are found to be distorted or invalid. As I will discuss in Chapter Five, this is the core component of transformative learning.

In this chapter, critical reflection has been defined so as to be congruent with transformative learning theory. It is useful, however, to see contrasting perspectives of the concept, such as King and Kitchener's reflective judgment model (1994) and Schön's exploration of reflective practice (1983). Mezirow (1991) distinguished between content, process, and premise reflection in order to differentiate transformative learning from nonreflective learning.

When educator development is viewed as critically reflective learning, it casts a different light on how we describe that process. It is no longer a matter of improving techniques but rather a way of understanding why we do what we do and changing our practice if it has been based on invalid or constraining habits.

Educator development that incorporates critical reflection results in educators' articulating the assumptions that underlie their practice, determining the sources and consequences of those assumptions, critically questioning the assumptions, and imagining alternatives to their current perspective on practice. Some workshops and other professional development activities may be designed to promote aspects of critical reflection. Educators may have experienced the use of critical incidents, role plays, simulations, or repertory grids in this context. However, as I discussed in Chapter Two, when the workshop or retreat is over, the reflection process that was begun may take a back seat to the pressures of everyday practice. It is critical that educators involve themselves in ongoing reflective developmental work. To this end, I have suggested strategies that educators might use individually, with a colleague or friend, or in a small group to foster critical reflection.

Chapter Five

Becoming a Transformative Learner

In Chapters Three and Four, I discussed self-directed learning as a foundation of transformative learning, and critical reflection as a central process involved in transformative learning. I suggested practical strategies for educators to use in their development. Real change and growth in our practice is an ongoing process of examining and questioning our assumptions, values, and perspectives. We need to move beyond "tinkering with teaching" and consider our fundamental beliefs and philosophies.

Over the past two decades, Jack Mezirow has developed his theory of transformative learning. It is my belief that his work has marked a significant change in the adult education literature. His thinking is now beginning to have a strong impact on practitioners. Researchers' and writers' interest in the process of transformative learning is also increasing (for example, see Dirkx and others, 1993; Tennant, 1993; Schlattner, 1994). The theory has not yet been directly applied to educators as learners; this is my intent here.

In this chapter, I describe the fundamental concepts of transformative learning theory in relation to educator development. What meaning perspectives on education do adult educators hold? What are some common distortions in those perspectives? How do our psychological, sociolinguistic, and epistemic meaning perspectives relate to our practice as educators? How is becoming self-directed as an educator a transformative process in itself? How can the critical reflection processes discussed in Chapter Four lead to transformed practice?

Meaning Perspectives on Being an Adult Educator

A meaning perspective is defined as "a habitual set of expectations that constitutes an orienting frame of reference that we use in projecting our symbolic models and that serves as a (usually tacit) belief system for interpreting and evaluating the meaning of experience" (Mezirow, 1991, p. 42). Meaning perspectives can be described as filters, frameworks, or paradigms that shape our perceptions of ourselves, others, and our surroundings. Meaning perspectives are formed through experiences. One's past experience shapes the way one assimilates new experiences.

As I discussed in Chapter One, most of our interests and knowledge about educational practice are practical (concerned with mutual understanding) and emancipatory (concerned with self-awareness) in nature rather than technical (concerned with the control and manipulation of the environment). That is, there are few objective truths, black-and-white issues, or definite cause-and-effect relationships. Consequently, an awareness of our meaning perspectives as educators becomes critical to our development. These perspectives shape understanding and learning; we need to be aware of them and have them open to questioning.

Within the broader perspectives on practice, we have specific sets of knowledge, beliefs, value judgments, feelings, and assumptions. Mezirow (1991, p. 44) labels these more concrete manifestations of perspectives as *meaning schemes*. In Chapter Four, in the discussion of critical reflection, I was primarily looking at strategies for articulating and questioning meaning schemes rather than meaning perspectives. Mezirow (1991, p. 44) argues that meaning schemes are "much more likely to be examined critically and transformed by reflection than meaning perspectives." To illustrate, if an educator holds a perspective on the role of educators as powerful figures of authority and expertise, he or she might then hold a set of interrelated beliefs about what an educator should do, such as determining the agenda, presenting the information, and evaluating the learning. These actions would be evidence of specific meaning schemes, all of which fit into the overall perspective on educators' roles.

Epistemic Perspectives

Epistemic meaning perspectives pertain to knowledge—what we know, how we have come to know it, and how we use the knowledge. Mezirow (1991) lists several factors that shape epistemic perspectives: developmental stage, cognitive or learning styles, sensory learning preferences, scope of awareness, criteria used for evaluation or judgment, global versus detail focus, and concrete or abstract thinking, among others. Some of these factors may lead to constraints or distortions in knowledge; for example, if a person has a preference for focusing on details and facts, she or he may not have a grasp of the larger picture.

Epistemic meaning perspectives on being an adult educator include knowledge about the teaching and learning process, how a person came to have that knowledge, and the way the knowledge is used or acted upon. Two illustrations of individuals with quite different epistemic meaning perspectives will be used to make these concepts more concrete.

Judi is a counselor and an educator. She works individually with clients who have experienced abuse in childhood. She also holds two separate series of educational groups for victims and for offenders, the participants being referred to her by the courts. Judi's formal education consists of college training for the nursing profession. She worked as a staff nurse briefly, realized that it did not suit her, moved to a social service agency, and from there moved to a counseling practice. Judi has no formal education as a counselor or an educator but continually attends workshops, group discussions, and seminars. She is also an avid reader of a wide variety of counseling and educational books, journals, and newsletters. Every time I see Judi she is full of enthusiasm for a new theory or strategy relevant to her practice. Judi describes her epistemic meaning perspective on being an educator:

> I don't see much difference between education and counseling; they are both helping people to grow as people. I know that I couldn't go to university anymore and sit in a lecture; it doesn't interest me to sit and listen to someone talk about some abstract thing. I suppose I should. I should have a degree. But at my stage

of life, I don't think I could do it. I don't have a real framework for being an educator. I do what works, and I know what will work with which group. I couldn't hang it all onto one model. I don't think it is like that. I take a piece from here, a piece from there. I go to a workshop and I think, "Hey, that's a good idea" and I try it, but I may adapt it, and I may not buy the whole theory that it's based on. I know lots of different strategies and techniques, but I would have trouble telling you why I use one and not the other in a particular session. My knowledge is intuitive. I do not do too much analysis of it.

Can we see Judi's epistemic meaning perspective? Is she aware of her own philosophy of practice? It seems that she is partly conscious and partly not conscious of what she knows. She has a clear awareness of how she prefers to learn. Her underlying philosophy is similar to Schön's conceptualization of reflection-in-action (1983).

George's educational background includes two formal degrees, a bachelor's and a master's in education. At the undergraduate level, George went through a high school teacher training program, but after a short time working with high school students he decided this profession did not suit him, and he went back to the university. He now teaches education at the college level. His students have diverse career goals, including being early-childhood educators or teacher aides. When I asked George about his practice, he revealed that he was familiar with Mezirow's work. Here is a part of his response.

I would say that my practice is informed by Dewey's work; I have long been a student of Dewey's writing. I see encouraging critical reflection, teaching problem-solving skills, and incorporating experiential learning activities into my teaching as best describing my goals as an educator.

I see myself as an expert in educational theory. I believe that it is my job to set the standards in my classes, to challenge my students, and to judge the quality of their work. Sometimes my students complain that the readings are too difficult or that they are not relevant to their interests, but I challenge them to stretch beyond their expectations. I do not agree with the approaches advocated by adult educators where everyone "does their own thing" and then evaluates what they did. I am a teacher because I have more experience and I know more than my students and it is my responsibility to use that expertise.

How do I learn? I learn by reading and thinking and writing. I then share that expertise with my students. I also believe in an open and caring approach. I want my students to love learning and to love teaching. They can then share this love of learning with their own students.

What can we say about George's epistemic perspectives? He has a well-developed and well-articulated knowledge of educational practice. Does he know how he obtained that knowledge? From this excerpt, we might say that this is less clear. We return to George's case in the next section.

Sociolinguistic Perspectives

Sociolinguistic meaning perspectives pertain to social norms, cultural codes, and the way we use language. We tend to be unaware of the influence of the factors that shape sociolinguistic perspectives, for example, language games, secondary socialization, ethnocentrism, prototypes, and scripts (Mezirow, 1991). How such factors distort our perspectives is discussed in the next section.

Sociolinguistic meaning perspectives on being an educator are diverse and wide-ranging. They may be related to how we see the roles of educators and learners in society, how we see the role of education in general, our perception of the relationship between work and learning, or our conception of the political dimensions of learning and education. The educator who grew up in a working-class community where education was devalued may have different perspectives than the educator whose parents were educators themselves. The educator who completed her own formal learning in India may have different perspectives than the educator who studied in Canada. However, there clearly can be no *predictable* patterns of the influence of cultural background on meaning perspectives.

To illustrate, let us return to Judi and George from the previous section and examine some excerpts from their descriptions of their sociolinguistic perspectives on being an educator.

Judi's practice centers on helping people who have been adversely influenced by family norms, if not social norms as well. She uses the concepts of prototypes and scripts in her work with clients, so she had no difficulty with the idea of sociolinguistic perspectives. She did have some trouble applying it to her perspective of herself as an educator.

> I grew up in a strongly religious family. Working hard was the primary value for boys and taking care of others the best thing girls could do. This was the value of the church and of the community, and the women took second place.

> So, how does that describe my educator role? It's the opposite, almost. I was driving myself crazy as a counselor trying to take care of people, running to their rescue in the middle of the night, all sorts of ridiculous things. I had to stop doing that. I started thinking of myself as an educator rather than a rescuer. So being an educator was breaking with that early pattern. I know it is still 'helping,' but it is less 'taking care of.'

> I guess I am also influenced by all the usual North American values on education. I value it, I wish I had more, I feel guilty that I don't.

We all tend to take social norms for granted. What can we learn from Judi's comments here? She is aware of the influence of social norms, both from her past and in a more global sense. Does she describe her perspective on being an educator only from within that framework, or is she aware of alternatives? When the goal is transformative learning, the building blocks (meaning schemes) of that framework (perspective) need to be opened up for questioning. This may be the next step for Judi.

George is familiar with the basic concepts of transformative learning theory, as mentioned earlier. However, he too had some difficulty in describing his sociolinguistic meaning perspective on being an educator. Some excerpts:

> I'm an American working in a Canadian university. Even though I've been here for quite some time, I see that my cultural background is different than that of my colleagues. As an educator? I am less conservative, more interested in doing things, I'm probably louder, I fight for my ideals.

I grew up in a community that valued education. But they valued using that education to make money. So, being a teacher is really against the values from my background. That may explain why I do a lot of consulting—trying to assuage the guilt of not living up to expectations, perhaps.

I see the role of education in society being one of contributing to democracy. I see education as a political activity; it is only through education that we can create the freedom to participate in a democratic society.

What can we see in George's comments? He described some important ways in which his perspective on being an educator was influenced by his cultural background. And of course he used that perspective to describe how he saw education and his role in it.

Psychological Perspectives

Psychological meaning perspectives pertain to our understanding of ourselves as individuals. If a person describes herself as capable or as lacking in self-confidence, these are aspects of a psychological perspective. Factors that shape psychological perspectives may include, for example, self-concept, locus of control, tolerance of ambiguity, inhibitions, defense mechanisms, or characterological preferences (Mezirow, 1991). I would add psychological type preferences (see Chapter Six) to this list.

Psychological perspectives on being an educator may be difficult to differentiate from sociolinguistic or epistemic perspectives, as being an educator is a social role and one that involves acquiring and using knowledge. However, the way we view ourselves as people is a deeply woven strand in the fabric of our perspectives on the educator role. Examples of psychological perspectives related to being an educator might include seeing oneself as a caring person, feeling anxious about not having enough experience, being afraid of failing, seeing oneself as an extraverted intuitive type of person, or fearing losing control over learners. Most psychological perspectives would apply to several or all aspects of a person's life (such as seeing oneself as a caring person); others may be more specific to the educator role (fear of losing control of learners) and derived directly from past educational experiences.

Articulating and working with psychological meaning perspectives is the basis of psychoanalysis (for example, see Gould, 1990) and counseling (Mezirow, 1991). Clearly, this is a difficult process; it is easier to talk about what one knows or one's background than to describe personal fears and private perceptions of oneself. We will continue following the illustrations provided by Judi and George; both struggled with this question even though Judi is a counselor and quite comfortable with expressing personal perspectives.

An excerpt from Judi's description of her psychological perspective on being an educator follows.

> I'm truly a caring person. I don't think there's anything wrong with that if I don't overdo it, and that is a part of my strength as an educator. I can connect with people, reach them intuitively. Yes, I'm an intuitive person and a feeling person, and those pertain to my view of myself as an educator as well as to most of the rest of my life.

> I never think I know enough, but that's more related to knowledge? My self-concept as a person is OK, but not my self-concept as an educator.

> I'm just starting to learn to be myself, to free myself from the strong constraints of my background. That part of it is social, I know, but the dysfunctional dependence was psychological, and I think that influenced my view of myself as a professional and an educator.

What could we say about Judi's psychological perspective on being an educator? She was able to distinguish some parts of her psychological perspective that were intertwined with the other domains, but nevertheless related to her personal view of herself. She could also connect these views to herself as educator.

George was less in touch with the relationship between himself as a person and as an educator; perhaps he also had less experience at articulating psychological perspectives. Among other views, he provided the following:

> I try to be an authentic person when I work with my students. I think I am myself. I express a strong individuality. I believe that it is critical to be open and honest and have everyone feel free to express his or her views.

Things about myself as a person that have an impact on my view of myself as an educator? That's a hard one. I told you that I value education.

Actually none of my students really *know* me, me as a person, now that I think about your question. As a teacher, I have a job to do, responsibilities, I'm not there to "share" myself or get into a 1960s encounter group. Sometimes after a class I go to my office and lie flat on the floor to recover myself, to gain my own equilibrium, so I can see that I'm playing a role. But I believe that's what I should be doing. Otherwise, why not invite everyone for supper and to meet the kids and talk about the weather?

How does George understand his psychological perspective? He begins by describing himself as authentic and then discusses the roles he plays. Do we tend to separate our professional selves from our personal selves? To some extent, George does this, but perhaps his description illustrates in part the nature of his psychological meaning perspectives on being an educator and how they are related to his personal perspectives.

In the next section, we see how each type of perspective can be distorted. What are the ways in which our perspectives are formed? How do they become limited or constrained? How can we go on to revise or transform our perspectives on our practice as educators?

Distortions in Meaning Perspectives

Perhaps Mezirow would have been more accurate to use the term "undeveloped" meaning perspectives, rather than "distorted" meaning perspectives. The term *distortion* often leads people to question, "Who can tell me that my way of seeing things is distorted?" Mezirow (1991, p. 188) writes: "A distorted assumption or premise is one that leads the learner to view reality in a way that arbitrarily limits what is included, impedes differentiation, lacks permeability or openness to other ways of seeing, or does not facilitate an integration of experience." He is clear in saying that the term distortion includes "perspectives of adults that have not been fully developed" (Mezirow, 1991, p. 119). It is a matter of being unaware that we have made an assumption and being unaware that that assumption could be questioned that constrains our vision. When we are unaware, we have no choice. It is not that perspectives are right or wrong but rather that they may not have been made conscious and open to critical reflection. When this is the case, we have limited our freedom of choice. It is for this reason that Brookfield (1987) argues that critical thinking is a cornerstone of democracy.

Our sociocultural context is significant in shaping our perspectives. Jarvis (1992b, p. 23) suggests that when people develop, they "begin to act back on the social world that has formed them." He sees learning as both a process of conforming to the social world and one of generating social change (see Chapter Seven). Sometimes though, sociocultural forces, driven by those in power in our organizations, create contexts in which the individual can do little to change what is valued. This too needs to be recognized when we question our perspectives.

Distorted Epistemic Perspectives

There are several ways in which people can be limited by what they know, how they come to know, and how they use knowledge:

- Operating at an early stage in the development of reflective judgment where controversies do not exist (King and Kitchener, 1994)
- Being influenced by perceptual filters, such as attention to detail, narrowness of focus, or discernment of patterns (Roth, 1990)
- Being unable to utilize different dimensions of cognitive style, such as considering alternatives, construing the world in a multidimensional way, or categorizing concepts (Knox, 1977)
- Being unable to go through a learning cycle using each of the styles that form that cycle (such as active experimentation, reflective observation, concrete experience, and abstract conceptualization) (Kolb, 1984)
- Being limited in one's perception of what knowledge is (rational, values-based, factual, or potential) by virtue of one's psychological type (Cranton, 1994a)

What does this mean in terms of educators' limitations in their epistemic perspectives? Many adult educators do not have formal preparation for their roles (Brockett, 1991a) and therefore tend to teach in the way they were taught. Their knowledge of educational practice is limited to their own experiences. All educators are limited by their preferred way of learning and the way they use their knowledge. Distorted epistemic perspectives might include

- Seeing teaching effectiveness as a black-and-white issue, whereby one method or technique is more likely to lead to learning than another
- Being influenced by perceptual filters and therefore concentrating on details or having a narrow focus on the teaching and learning process
- Being limited by adhering to one dimension or another of cognitive style, for example, not seeing the multidimensional nature of being an educator
- Staying with one's preferred learning style, for example, seeing concrete experience as the only or the best way to learn
- Being restricted by one's preferred psychological type, for example, viewing the teaching and learning process as a logical rational one
- Adopting as one's own the knowledge of a powerful leader, an expert, or an organizational philosophy

It is difficult, if not impossible, to discover such limits or distortions by oneself. When you are unaware of a limitation, how do you go about finding it? As was discussed in Chapter Four, interaction and discussion with others can raise awareness of distorted assumptions.

Distorted Sociolinguistic Perspectives

Distortions of sociolinguistic perspectives are the products of "all the mechanisms by which society and language arbitrarily shape and limit our perception and understanding, such as implicit ideologies; language games; cultural codes; social norms, roles, and practices; and underdeveloped levels of consciousness, as well as theories and philosophies. All contain values and behavioral expectations, and all are implemented through 'recipe' knowledge" (Mezirow, 1991, pp. 130–131). The ways in which sociolinguistic

distortions occur are almost limitless, especially as the communications technology explosion has dramatically increased individuals' exposure to media systems. I recently saw satellite dishes leased
to Tennessee hill people who could not calculate the monthly cost.

Writers and researchers have provided strong arguments and
good evidence as to the influence of media on our perspectives
(see Brookfield, 1990b; McLaren, 1991). But this is just one set of
factors that influence our perspectives. Some others follow.

- The way we use language. By labeling people, objects, or
  events in a particular way, we may give to something more or
  less power than it has, or give it characteristics that go with the
  label rather than the person or object. One example is the use
  of the word "baby" in reference to a woman.
- Metaphors. We use metaphors without consciousness; yet they
  have the power to shape our perceptions. When we describe
  learners as "blank slates" or "sponges," we are expressing a
  strong image of a perspective on the learning process.
- Reification. Systems such as legal systems, government systems,
  and educational systems become powerful forces which no
  person feels free to question. The legal system just "is"; people
  talk of "they" without a knowledge of who "they" are. In this
  way we are influenced to follow, without question, certain
  norms and procedures that we assume to be unchangeable.
- Power. Individuals, organizations, and sociocultural forces may
  have a strong influence on our perspectives of practice. Jarvis
  (1992b, p. 233), in writing about the political dimensions of
  learning, suggests that when people have power exercised over
  them their learning may be constrained by those in power.

This is but a sample of distorting influences on sociolinguistic
perspectives. Let us turn to how educators might be limited by
their sociolinguistic perspectives. Education is, in itself, a system
that has sets of cultural and social norms. We speak of teachers
being "socialized," meaning that they learn to behave like other
teachers and work within the system. Kincheloe (1991) sees that
the "professional training which emerges is obsessed with format
over substance, with teaching teachers to be 'supervisable', to be
team players, to fit into organizational structures" (p. viii). Educa-

tors are often working within a strong, unquestioned educational culture which is, in turn, within the broader cultures of community and country. Examples of limiting or distorted sociolinguistic perspectives are

- Not questioning media portrayals of education or the roles of educators in society
- Using language in a way that conveys unquestioned assumptions about the roles of educators and learners (even the use of the words *teacher* and *student* describes a power differential that may not exist in adult education settings)
- Unconsciously using metaphors to describe learners, educators, or the learning process that convey certain images (I once heard an adult educator refer to her group as "kids")
- Seeing the educational system (whether it be college, university, business, industry, or school) as not open to question or challenge
- Feeling constrained by the "system" as an educator
- Feeling obligated to become socialized into the organizational structure

Distorted Psychological Perspectives

Mezirow (1991) sees distorted psychological perspectives as primarily the product of childhood experience. He writes that they "produce ways of feeling and acting that cause us pain because they are inconsistent with our self-concept or sense of how we want to be as adults" (p. 138). In this area, Mezirow uses the work of Gould (1989), a psychiatrist, to explain how childhood prohibitions block adult behaviors. Parents impose rules on children, rules which at the time are useful and necessary. When these prohibitions are learned in a traumatic context such as threat of withdrawal of love or physical punishment, the prohibition can come to block adult functioning. Autonomy is no longer possible; the individual has distorted psychological perspectives. Although this is a reasonable source of distortion, I would argue that limited or distorted psychological meaning perspectives are not only related to childhood events of this nature or solely to one's childhood. Possible sources of distorted or limited psychological perspectives include

- Being unconscious of the influences of childhood experiences on our psychological make-up. Individuals may not be aware of the nature of their relationship with parents or siblings or, if aware, may not have considered how these experiences have shaped their perspectives.
- Being unaware of psychological preferences. People tend to assume that all others see the world as they do and may not be aware of individual differences in preferences for, say, logic-versus value-based decision making or introversion versus extraversion (see Chapter Six).
- Experiencing an abusive relationship. Whether as a child or as an adult, living in a relationship where one is abused can lead to an inability to see oneself in a valid way or to be open to questioning the nature of the self.
- Experiencing failure. Individuals who lose their jobs or perceive ongoing failure in their work are often said to "lose perspective." The ability to interpret and evaluate the meaning of the experience is reduced.
- Experiencing loss. The loss of a spouse, parent, child, or other loved one can lead to the same inability to interpret and evaluate experiences.
- Experiencing joy. People can be equally prone to distortion in personal perspectives from experiencing unexpected or not-understood positive events. The chaos produced in the lives of some lottery winners serves as one example of this.

Individuals react in very different ways to trauma of any kind. Also, sources of distortion may interact with each other in different ways for individuals of varying natures. If I have a low tolerance of ambiguity and if I am in a prolonged ambiguous situation, I may lose my ability to maintain my perspective or, in other words, to see and question myself. The same situation may have no impact on another individual.

We saw earlier that educators' psychological perspectives on their practice may be a subset of their more general and personal psychological perspectives. Distortions or limitations for educators could include some of the following:

- Being unaware of the influence of a childhood experience on one's perception of oneself as an educator; for example, having an early negative experience as a student and behaving, as an educator, in a way that is related to that experience

- Being unaware of one's teaching or learning style preferences, or unconsciously teaching in the way that one would like to be taught
- Having experienced failure or perceived failure in one's practice, such as receiving ongoing poor evaluation results without an understanding of why, and seeing this as a personal flaw
- Having lost one's job and perceived this as a personal failure

Each of these examples is fairly general. One can imagine any number of specific incidents for individuals that could lead to a limiting of psychological perspectives. Any event or situation that leads an individual to be unable to question his or her interpretation of that experience contributes to a limited perspective.

Developing Self-Direction as a Transformative Process

In Chapter Three, I discussed strategies educators could use to engage in self-directed development. Using Candy's four-faceted model of self-directed learning (1991), I described these strategies in terms of developing personal autonomy, managing one's own education, making decisions about learning within formal settings, and pursuing learning projects outside of an institution.

Autonomy means self-rule and was originally used to describe self-ruled cities in Ancient Greece. Today it is used, in conversation, to mean freedom or independence. In the literature, many people have defined autonomy, from both philosophical (Dearden, 1972) and psychological perspectives (Erikson, 1959; Weathersby, 1981). It is alternately seen to be an innate disposition (Rogers, 1969), something learned through education (Wang, 1983), or a product of development (Weathersby, 1981).

As adult educators, we tend to take a fairly eclectic view of autonomy. Candy (1991) and Tennant and Pogson (1995) draw together a variety of perspectives in their discussions of autonomy. It may be, in part, a disposition or personality trait; autonomy may increase as people mature and develop; and we hope that we can foster autonomy through education.

Returning to the broader concept of self-directed learning, most individuals display self-direction in various aspects of their personal and professional lives: managing finances, raising children, making career decisions, running a household. However, many of us associate education and learning with being taught. As students, we see ourselves as having decisions made for us by experts and as passively listening or watching while someone else gives us the content. Becoming self-directed learners of our practice can involve reconsidering and perhaps changing our beliefs and assumptions about education; in other words, it can be transformative learning. This may be more likely for educators as learners than for learners in other contexts.

Jarvis (1992b) discusses self-directed learning in relation to control over the space in which people act, be it delegated or owned (p. 132), and connects this in turn with people's desire to exercise free will. It is this distinction between delegated and owned space that leads me to suggest that becoming self-directed may be more difficult for educators than for other learners. When someone attends a course or a workshop in which the control is delegated to him or her, becoming self-directed is a matter of learning how to use that control to make decisions about the learning. Jarvis (1992b, p. 133) states that "where control is delegated, self-directed learning is a teaching technique rather than a learning strategy." It is when a person owns or controls the space to begin with, and also has a desire to exercise free will, that autonomy can develop. Most educators have control over the space in which they act; that is, whether to learn about their practice or not is their decision. It may be that becoming autonomous or autodidactic has a greater potential to be transformative learning than does developing learner-controlled or self-management strategies.

What are these processes for adult educators? In traditional development strategies (see Chapter Two), the space is controlled by others. Educators attend workshops or read newsletters in which experts provide them with tips, techniques, or strategies to try in their own classrooms. Educators have come to expect this approach as it falls within their perspective on what education is. Self-management (choosing which workshops to attend) is the only form self-direction takes, and educators are satisfied with this.

If it should happen that educators attend a session where the facilitator delegates control to participants (the learner-control dimension of self-directed learning), there may be resistance. They have come to hear from an expert. Delahaye, Limerick, and Hearn (1994) argue that pedagogy and andragogy are orthogonal (independent) concepts, thereby allowing the possibility of "high pedagogy" and "high andragogy" in one stage of learning. Although the authors do not comment on this interpretation of their results, participants in their study actually saw the concepts of pedagogy and andragogy as mutually exclusive. This in turn implies people would see a movement from instructor-centered or subject-oriented learning to self-directed learning as an important transition. Such a shift in perspective could be transformative.

It is in the areas of personal autonomy and autodidaxy, however, where becoming a self-directed learner of educational practice is most likely to be a transformative process. The definition of personal autonomy is troublesome, and the extent to which autonomy can be deliberately learned is questionable. Jarvis (1992b, pp. 141–142) points out that "while the ideology of society is that people are free and autonomous, a great deal of human learning is other-directed and certainly other-controlled." Yet as adult educators, we have probably all witnessed the development of personal autonomy in some individuals with whom we have worked.

Candy (1991) makes three arguments: that autonomy is an innate disposition, that autonomy develops over time in response to experience and socialization, and that autonomy can be learned. Although he describes these as three "*alternative* points of view" (p. 115, emphasis added), it is quite possible that all three perspectives are valid. Candy also describes autonomy as a process rather than a product; in other words, one does not simply become autonomous, but rather one thinks, feels, or acts autonomously in some contexts. If this is accepted as a part of the definition, one can see that autonomy is a part of educators' character, that it develops naturally with teaching experience, and that educators can set out to become more autonomous in relation to their practice. Candy writes that "an autonomous person is able to assent to rules, or modify or reject them, if they are found wanting" (1991, p. 113). The autodidactic process (the independent pursuit of learning) would be one means by which educators would demonstrate and gain autonomy in their development as practitioners.

The educator who is able to assent to rules, modify, or reject them is an educator who is open to questioning and modifying his or her own assumptions, values, and beliefs about practice. We have the notion of becoming self-directed as a transformative process, and we have been engaging in transformation as developing personal autonomy. An illustration may be helpful here.

Veronica is a native Micmac who lives and works with Micmac students on a reservation in Canada. Although her course is called "Lifeskills," Veronica works with a variety of concepts and often teaches literacy skills as well. She is particularly sensitive to the preservation of native values and native spirituality—therefore she resents and deviates considerably from the curriculum she is given by the government.

Veronica had no formal teacher training, but she recently embarked on a certificate in adult education at a university several hours' drive from her home. The courses were partly done via distance education, and Veronica came to the city for the summer sessions.

Veronica has gained self-management skills; she selects her courses, participates in the planning of her program, and is very interested in obtaining the certificate in adult education. Until recently she would not have described herself as "autonomous" or as "becoming autonomous." Personal autonomy is not a social norm for Veronica, and she is very aware of the lack of political autonomy her people have.

Veronica enrolled in an elective course on self-directed and transformative learning. It was assumed that she would take full responsibility for her learning projects. There were no requirements and no expectations given. Veronica spent the first half of the summer session trying to understand the situation she found herself in. Through her readings and discussions with others, she came to grasp the various aspects of self-directed learning and began to feel comfortable with learner control.

It is not until several weeks later, when Veronica was back in her practice, that she began to question her values as an educator and to engage in a process of moving toward autonomy as an educator. This process was stimulated by the introduction of a Caucasian supervisor into Veronica's workplace, a person critical of her methods and expertise. Veronica went back to her readings from her course, reflected on her practice, questioned her strategies, and began to see herself as a reformer. This led her to further independent study and reading, discussions with her learners, and plans to change the system within which she was working. Veronica still objects to the phrase "personal autonomy," but she acknowledges the transformative nature of her experience.

How can we understand Veronica's experience? In her practice, she was fairly autonomous, modifying the given curriculum to match her perceptions of the context within which she worked. Her cultural context is one in which individual autonomy is valued less than political autonomy, so Veronica did not accept the notion of individual autonomy. As a learner, she went through a process of becoming more self-directed but did not apply this to her practice as an educator until an external constraint (a new supervisor) led her to reflect on her work style. We see, in Veronica's story, the intertwined nature of self-directed and transformative learning.

Critical Reflection Leading to Transformation

In Chapter Four, I discussed various approaches to reflection as well as strategies for educators who wish to engage in critical reflection on their practice. These include ways of articulating assumptions about practice, strategies for understanding where our assumptions come from and what their consequences might be, guidelines for critical questioning of assumptions, and ways of imagining alternatives to what we believe.

Critical reflection can lead to changes in one's perspective on practice, or it can serve to confirm current practices. Mezirow states clearly that not all reflection leads to transformative learning: "it may result in an elaboration, confirmation, or creation of a scheme" (1991, p. 108). He also points out that "[n]ot all adult education involves reflective learning; however, fostering reflective and transformative learning should be the cardinal goal of adult education" (Mezirow, 1991, p. 117). It is only when a revision of basic assumptions, beliefs, or a perspective on education takes place that a transformation has occurred. If the process of reflection leads to an awareness of an invalid, undeveloped, or distorted meaning scheme or perspective; if that scheme or perspective is then revised; and if the educator acts on the revised belief, the development has been transformative.

How can we ensure that educator development contains transformative learning? This is not to say that the learning of new schemes or the confirmation of old schemes is not also valuable learning; but on the other hand, it is clear that our most profound learning experiences are transformative. Newman (1994) nicely summarizes the shifting place of reflection in adult education over the past twenty-five years, pointing out how reflection became separated from action. Boud and Walker (1992), for example, argue that during reflection the learner is by definition detached from the experience. However, Mezirow has recontextualized the act of reflection (Newman, 1994, p. 239). In other words, for perspective transformation to occur, we not only examine the content of our experiences, but we question why we are questioning (premise reflection). It is that process that distinguishes transformative from normative learning.

Mezirow (1994) points out that "most adult education has been devoted to a description of how to facilitate instrumental learning" (p. 226). As we saw in Chapter Two, most traditional educator development has also been focused on instrumental learning. Reflection, on the other hand, can be defined as attending to the grounds or justification for one's beliefs (Mezirow, 1994). And, "[r]eflective action often involves overcoming situational, knowledge, and emotional constraints" (Mezirow, 1994, p. 226). If educators are to turn their reflection on their practice into transformative learning about their practice, some or all of the following conditions will need to be in place:

- The old ways of seeing practice simply do not work
- A "disorienting dilemma" exists
- The origin of beliefs is critically examined
- There are others with whom discourse can be held
- The educator is ready for change
- Freedom from constraints can be achieved
- Support is available
- An alternative way of being is possible

Elsewhere, I have suggested practical strategies for promoting and supporting transformative learning in others (Cranton, 1994a): critical questioning, journal writing, consciousness-raising exercises, and experiential activities. Educators can deliberately apply such strategies to turn critical reflection on their practice into transformative learning.

The following illustration may be helpful.

Glen is involved in the administration of a distance education project in the Maritime Provinces of Canada. In working toward an M.Ed. degree in adult education, he participated in a course on self-directed and transformative learning over a summer session. Glen decided to keep a journal for the duration of the course, relating concepts and ideas discussed among the participants to his own practice as an educator. In his journal, Glen reflected on his past experiences as an educator in order to understand the origins of his beliefs about his practice.

Initially, the journal contained descriptions of Glen's thoughts on what we discussed in class and stories of his own experiences. However, in one installment, he told a story that demanded questioning. He had spent one year teaching in a high school in a remote area, and that year was probably the worst of his life. The students were aggressive and even violent; he had no way of "controlling" them, and he had no support from the school administration. Quite the opposite, in fact: Glen felt as harassed by the school principal as by the students. He left that position at the end of the year with great relief, thinking that he was not meant to be a teacher.

Glen was first unable to see past the content of his experience. With critical questioning from others in the group, Glen began to relate this experience to his parents' expectations of him, to his own personal need for structure and order, and to his social expectations about others' behavior. Glen was open to questioning and willing to engage in discourse about his experience even though he was a rather introverted person. By the end of our course, Glen was beginning to see his practice as an educator in a "whole new light." He saw himself, in the past experience, as being not open to others' ways of seeing things and as not being open to any deviation from the order and structure that he needed personally. He saw his current involvement in distance education as a reaction to that experience. The process was only beginning when our course ended and Glen left the university to return home, but perhaps the transformation of his perspective on his educator roles was under way.

Summary

Educators interpret their experiences so as to make meaning out of them. In transformation theory, these meaning structures are called meaning perspectives—broad frameworks or paradigms which determine our expectations of future experiences—and meaning schemes—the specific beliefs, assumptions, values, and concepts that make up general perspectives. Mezirow (1991) describes three types of perspectives. Educators have knowledge about teaching and learning and ways of gaining that knowledge: their epistemic perspectives. They are influenced by social norms, cultural codes, and language: their sociolinguistic perspectives. And educators have an understanding of themselves as individuals: their psychological perspectives.

Naturally enough, our perspectives can be undeveloped, not thought through clearly, constrained by the experiences we have had, or distorted by misinformation. Adult educators often come to their profession via paths that do not include preparation as an educator. They also may not identify with the profession of education, but rather with their subject area or the profession of the individuals they work with. As discussed in Chapter One, adult educators do not form a cohesive group. These factors can be relevant in limiting our perspectives on education.

Learning and development for us adult educators can be a process of questioning our beliefs about and perspectives on our practice. In order to do this, educators need to view their development as a self-directed endeavor. However, educators are often not used to self-directed learning, having learned their subject area in an other-directed fashion and having adopted an expert model themselves. Hence, becoming self-directed can be, in itself, a transformation of a perspective on education.

The central process of transformative learning is critical reflection—not detached reflection on past experience, but reflective action and reflecting on why we are reflecting. Not all reflection leads to transformation. Sometimes we confirm or consolidate our beliefs. Sometimes we learn something new. Both are valuable outcomes of reflection. However, transformative learning is a goal of adult education, and adult educators are adult learners. Mezirow (1994, p. 226) writes: "Adult development means the progressive realization of an adult's capacity to fully and freely participate in rational dialogue, to achieve a broader, more discriminating, permeable and integrative understanding of his/her experience as a guide to action." This is the essence of professional development for educators.

Chapter Six

Individual Differences in Educator Development

I have described educators' growth and development as a process of becoming more autonomous, of reflecting critically on practice, and of revising perspectives on practice. All educators can attest to the differences they observe among individuals in a learning group. Some prefer logical and well-organized activities, others are more interested in getting to know the people in the group; some want to hear the facts, others are drawn to the big picture. The popularity of the concept of learning styles and the way these style descriptions seem to "ring true" are indicative of the importance we give to individual differences. Although we readily accept the varying preferences of our learners, we are less likely to apply this knowledge to ourselves.

Educators also learn and develop in different ways. Some people learn by reading, others by talking; some educators love to go to conferences, others prefer to experiment in their own classroom. We may also prefer to learn assorted things in varying ways, for example, learning to manage the time in a workshop through experience, and learning about innovative approaches to group work through reading.

The stance that there is no one best way to learn and no one developmental path for all people is not simply a product of North American individualism. The notion that there is a multiplicity of meanings and that individuals have their own unique interpretations of reality comes to us through hermeneutics, the "discipline concerned with the investigation and interpretation of human behavior, speech, institutions . . . as essentially intentional" (Flew,

1984, p. 146). With the Age of Enlightenment and the desire to systematize all human knowledge through science, hermeneutics became the domain of philosophers.

Habermas, from whose work Mezirow drew, describes hermeneutics as concerning "itself with the experiences of the speaker" (Habermas, 1989, p. 298) in the dimension of language. He argues that through self-reflection, individuals become aware of unconscious presuppositions. He sees "hermeneutical consciousness [as] the result of a self-reflection in which the speaking subject becomes aware of his inherent freedoms and dependencies in regard to language" (p. 298). Each person's experiences and understanding of those experiences will be unique.

The tension between our technical interest in discovering scientific laws of human behavior and our practical interest in understanding each other and our social norms has always been strong. One of the most influential writers in this debate was Kelly (1955), who introduced his personal construct theory in response to the then-popular behaviorist theories and as an alternative to psychoanalytic theory. Kelly's fundamental postulate is that "a person's processes are psychologically channelized by the ways in which he anticipates events" (Kelly, 1963, p. 46). This basic assumption is elaborated through eleven corollaries, one of which is the individuality corollary: "Persons differ from each other in their construction of events" (Kelly, 1963, p. 55). Kelly acknowledges the role that a person plays in social processes and the commonalities among individuals, but he emphasizes that each person's construct system is unique. Adult educators, such as Candy (1991), drew on Kelly's work in order to understand how people learn.

The emphasis on individuality in the literature and in our culture can be questioned. Kelly's theory has been criticized along these lines (see Holland, 1970), as has Mezirow's transformative learning theory (Collard and Law, 1989; Clark and Wilson, 1991). In Chapter Seven, I address some of these concerns by examining educator development in organizational, cultural, and societal contexts.

The adult education literature has a tradition of understanding and promoting individual differences (Lindeman, 1926; Knowles, 1975). Mezirow (1991) explicitly bases transformative learning theory on constructivist thought. It is my intent in this chapter to examine educators' individual differences in becoming and being self-directed, in engaging in critical reflection, and in embarking on transformative learning about their practice.

The Potpourri of Individual Differences

It is the array of dimensions and factors by which individuals vary that makes instrumental knowledge about human behavior unobtainable. To begin with, no two people have exactly the same experiences in their lives, and we are assuming that past experiences influence our perception of current and anticipated experiences (Kelly, 1963; Mezirow, 1991). Beyond that fundamental difference among human beings, it has been postulated that people vary in learning style, teaching style, leadership style, personality characteristics, and social interaction preferences, to name but a few of the individual differences reported on in the literature. People also obviously have different values and cultural backgrounds, come from different communities, have a variety of educational backgrounds, and have different interests in and aptitudes for topics and skills.

In spite of the multitude of differences among people, the technical interest in explaining, predicting, and controlling led researchers and theorists to engage in many attempts to quantify and categorize human characteristics. For example, learning-styles inventories may tell us that we prefer to be accommodators, assimilators, convergers, or divergers (Kolb, 1984). One popular leadership-style assessment describes people as having strengths in telling (directive), selling (directive and supportive), participating (facilitating and communicating), or delegating (providing little direction or support) (Hersey and Blanchard, 1982). Another component of Hersey and Blanchard's theory involves defining four stages of maturity of followers: at the highest stage, people are both able and willing to do what is asked of them. We have measures of types, of critical thinking ability (Watson and Glaser, 1980), and of self-directed-learning readiness (Guglielmino, 1977).

Educator style has also been quantified and categorized, although to a lesser extent than learners' characteristics have. For example, Conti's Principles of Adult Learning Scale measures teaching style on a continuum from teacher-centered to student-centered (Conti, 1985). Heimlich and Norland (1994) present a teaching values inventory to help identify the extent to which educators value "content/curriculum, physical environment/resources, teacher/ method, learner community, and individual learner" (p. 36).

What are the criticisms of this approach? It is natural to want to describe ourselves and others so as to come to a better understanding of the learning process. However, if we believe that understanding human behavior is interpretive or constructivist, the quantification and categorization of individual differences, as in the above examples, could be misleading. First, it tends to be a one-way communication process; the educator or developer "tests" the learners and gives back the "results." Second, quantification can produce an aura of precision and objectivity where none exists. For example, the subjectivity of Hersey and Blanchard's notion (1982) that the highest stage of maturity of followers is demonstrated when people do as they are asked may go unquestioned because it is presented as an objective categorization system. Third, quantification or categorization encourages us to expect predictable relationships among characteristics where none may be possible. Candy (1991), among others, suggests that our understanding of adults in learning contexts best comes through qualitative inquiry. Kincheloe (1991) makes a powerful argument that our emphasis on quantitative methods and positivistic paradigms has adversely influenced the entire education system.

Nevertheless, it is not useful to discard the idea of "assessment." We continually assess ourselves and each other—through subjective judgment, through conversation, through observation, through reflection—to increase our self-awareness and our mutual understanding. Assessment of personal characteristics can take place in the interpretive and emancipatory paradigms. We may decide to respond to a set of questions or a checklist, determine the degree to which the results describe us, discuss our interpretation with others, question assumptions we have about ourselves, and come to a revised understanding of ourselves. It is this kind of process that I see as working hand-in-hand with transformative learning about educator practice. It is also this kind of understanding of individual differences that can be used to help us become sensitive to our varying developmental needs and styles.

In examining how transformative learning varies among individuals, I have used psychological type theory as a means of understanding people's differences (Cranton, 1994a). I believe that this framework is equally useful for describing educator development.

Psychological Type

Jung noticed patterns in the differences he observed among his clients in his psychoanalytic practice. As a psychoanalyst, a student of philosophy and literature, and a believer in concepts such as the collective unconscious, Jung was not tempted to objectify or quantify these differences. He argued that an observer of people must understand human behavior both objectively and subjectively. "The demand that he should see *only* objectively is quite out of the question, for it is impossible" (Jung, [1921] 1971, p. 9). The development of Jung's theory of psychological type took place over many years, always maintaining simultaneously the subjective and objective perspectives. It is for this reason that I believe psychological type theory can provide a powerful way of understanding individual differences while avoiding oversimplification of human nature.

Over the last six years, a colleague and I developed a procedure for assessing and interpreting psychological type profiles with individuals (Cranton and Knoop, 1995a). In over two thousand assessments, we found no two identical profiles, though we did observe the patterns and preferences referred to by Jung. I next briefly describe the theory and then relate it to educator development. For more detail, the reader should refer to Jung's original description ([1921] 1971) or Sharp's (1987) clear interpretation of the theory.

The Attitudes

Introversion and *extraversion* define the poles of a continuum for people's attitudes toward the world. Introversion is a preference for the subject, the self, or the inner world. Extraversion is a preference for the object, or the external world.

A tendency toward introversion is demonstrated by an interest in subjectifying experiences, events, or objects. Consequently, an introverted attitude may be interpreted as shyness, withdrawal, or a lack of social skills by an observer. The person may not appear to be in tune with reality, people, or events simply because he or she is more interested in the subjective world.

A tendency toward extraversion, on the other hand, is demonstrated by an interest in the world outside the self, including other people, experiences, events, and world happenings. The person may not appear to be reflective or self-aware simply because he or she is more interested in the external objective world.

All individuals display introverted and extraverted attitudes to varying degrees and in various combinations with what they are doing and where they are. It may be that someone is more extraverted at work and more introverted at home, or more extraverted when doing a certain kind of work and more introverted when engaged in another aspect of the job. Some people are equally comfortable being introverted and extraverted; other people have a strong preference for one attitude or the other.

Functions

The attitudes do not exist in isolation from other aspects of the psyche, although this was Jung's original conceptualization of psychological type. People have attitudes *toward* something—attitudes operate in conjunction with the functions of living.

Judgmental Functions

We make judgments and decisions continuously, including the small daily decisions about what to eat or wear, judgments as to whether we like or approve of something, and larger decisions about career options, financial matters, or personal relationships.

Jung describes two patterns or tendencies that people demonstrate in making judgments. The *thinking function* is revealed when people make logical, analytical judgments or decisions. A person might carefully weigh the advantages and disadvantages of two options before choosing one, or think through logically what should be done next.

The *feeling function* is revealed when judgments are made based on values, a subjective sense of acceptance or rejection, or a simple like-dislike criterion. A person might indicate a preference for one option or another without knowing why, or say that something just feels like the right decision.

Perceiving Functions

We make judgments about something, whether it be a movie, a car, or a job. To do this, we also perceive things, another function of living.

Again Jung observed two different patterns or preferences in the way individuals perceive the world around them. Use of the *sensing function* is demonstrated when a person uses his or her senses to perceive things. In examining a new car, meeting a person, listening to music, or eating a meal, the individual uses sight, touch, hearing, and taste to take in the qualities of the objects or people in the environment.

Use of the *intuitive function* is demonstrated when a person perceives things in an unconscious way, developing an image of the whole without using the senses, imagining what the object or person could be or could become, or seeing the possibilities for the object or person rather than the concrete observed reality. In meeting a person, viewing a painting, or examining a run-down building, the individual sees in his or her mind a whole image of what the person or object means to him or her.

Dominant, Auxiliary, and Inferior Functions

In his theory, Jung combines the two attitudes and the four functions in order to describe eight psychological types. He discusses the characteristics of extraverted thinking types, extraverted feeling types, introverted thinking types, and so on. Jung cautions us that these are neither rigid nor exclusive categories, but followers of Jung have fallen into the comfortable notion that we can objectively compartmentalize human characteristics. The most popular conceptualization of psychological type, that of Isabel Myers (1985), defines sixteen categories by combining the attitudes, one of the four functions as dominant, and one of the four functions as auxiliary. The formation of discrete categories of human behavior needs to be critically questioned and applied cautiously. I attempt to remain true to Jung's understanding of psychological type theory in the remainder of this discussion.

Jung argues that most people have a *dominant function*. That is, they have a preferred way of being. This may be a judgmental function (thinking or feeling, either introverted or extraverted) or a perceptive function (sensing or intuition, either introverted or extraverted). This does not mean that the person does not use the other functions, but rather that when there is choice in a situation, one function is preferred. If a person's dominant function is introverted thinking, her preference is to engage in inner contemplation of ideas. This does not mean that she cannot, or does not enjoy, discussions with others or social interactions. There is never just one way of being.

We all need to make judgments and to perceive things in order to survive in the world. If a person has a dominant judgmental function, he or she still perceives. The preferred perceptive function will be auxiliary or secondary to the dominant judgmental function. Almost all people, according to Jung, have a dominant and an auxiliary function. That is, they have a preferred way of making judgments and a preferred way of perceiving the world.

The dominant and the auxiliary functions can be introverted or extraverted. Perhaps most often, a person shows a general tendency to be introverted or extraverted, and both the dominant and the auxiliary functions are in the same attitude. However, people can have an extraverted dominant function and an introverted auxiliary function, or vice versa (Cranton and Knoop, 1995a). Jung does not address this issue directly. Myers (1985) measures introversion and extraversion in isolation from the functions, so this kind of profile cannot arise from her conceptualization of psychological type.

When a person has a strong dominant function, a clear preference for functioning in a certain way, then the opposite of that function is seldom used and becomes an *inferior function*. If I strongly prefer the thinking function and use that function whenever possible, I will rarely have an opportunity to use my feeling function. When situations arise that demand the use of a feeling function, I will be ill-equipped to deal with those situations. I might become agitated and make regrettable errors in my judgments. Similarly, a person whose dominant preference is for intuition—the perception of the whole and the possibilities it reveals—might make errors in the perception of concrete reality or the details of a situation.

Differentiation

So far, I have been describing people who have a clear preference for one function and a secondary preference for another function.

Such a profile would be called *differentiated;* in other words, there are demonstrable differences in the strength of preferences for functions. Jung refers to differentiation as "the development of differences, the separation of parts from a whole" ([1921] 1971, p. 424).

This is not the case for all individuals. Jung argues that "without differentiation direction is impossible, since the direction of a function towards a goal depends on the elimination of anything irrelevant" (pp. 424–425). Undifferentiation can lead a person to conflict in making judgments or in perceiving objects in the world. Lack of differentiation between the thinking and feeling functions can result in vacillation between logic and values as the basis for making a decision. Similarly, lack of differentiation between sensing and intuition can yield confusion in the interpretation of perceptions.

Self-Directed Development and Psychological Type

An understanding of individual preferences for the psychological attitudes and functions can enhance our sensitivity to our own developmental process as educators. If you enjoy discussion groups and conferences while I prefer to read articles and contemplate theories, we can both validate our choices of developmental strategies by being aware of our psychological natures.

In Chapter Three, self-directed learning about one's practice is presented as a goal; becoming self-directed is also described as a process—for some individuals, a process that could be transformative. In this section, I explore the relationships between psychological type preferences and inclinations toward the various facets of self-directed learning about practice.

Inclinations toward self-directed learning may be based on a variety of factors, including past experiences, cultural background, values, and underlying assumptions about teachers' roles. Let us speculate on how psychological type profiles could also be related to the way we choose to direct our learning and development. People who like to use their thinking function would enjoy organizing their own learning and would make logical decisions about the content or sequence of their development. If educators use the feeling function, they will be interested in working with others, working within social norms, and maintaining harmony with their surroundings. Use of the sensing function might focus the educator on facts, information, and concrete experiences in the learning process. A preference for the intuitive function can lead the educator to explore a wide variety of alternatives, to express divergent interests, and to follow his or her unique path through the learning process. One may predict that adopting an extraverted attitude will lead the educator to go "out there" to learn—workshops, conferences, courses, discussion groups. In the introverted attitude, a person might choose to read at home, to listen to tapes, to contemplate, and to reflect on past experiences.

The incorporation of psychological type theory into the research on adult learning is relatively new. There is some evidence that people with a preference for the intuitive function also prefer self-directed learning (Herbeson, 1992; Kreber, 1994). Unfortunately, these studies employed the Self-Directed Learning Readiness Scale (Guglielmino, 1977) and fall victim to the criticisms that can be leveled at this instrument (see Chapter Three). Using a qualitative approach, as one part of her doctoral thesis Tremblay (1981) asked people how they came to learn in a self-directed manner. Some of the responses were of a practical nature (time, convenience, and the like), but of those responses referring to personality traits, many could be related to a preference for the intuitive function (for example, creativity, yearning for freedom, and unwillingness to conform). Similarly, in an analysis of the experiences of ten autodidacts Danis and Tremblay (1985) conclude that the learning is unpredictable rather than linear or cyclical and that the individuals "take advantage of any opportunity that random events may offer them" (p. 139). Again, this description matches the characteristics of the intuitive function.

Candy (1991) provides a composite profile of the autonomous learner, containing over one hundred characteristics that have been linked with successful learning. Of these characteristics, thirty or nearly one-third of the list could be descriptors of an intuitive type. The second emphasis in Candy's profile is on thinking-type attributes: as examples, being able to analyze and plan, being logical and analytical, engaging in logical reasoning, and being reflective.

As a part of a larger study, a colleague and I asked 892 people, including nearly 500 educators, an open-ended question, "How do you prefer to learn?" (Cranton and Knoop, 1995b). Each participant also had completed the PET Type Check (Cranton and Knoop, 1995a) and had a psychological type profile based on their responses. We determined participants' dominant function, and where it was unclear we left the person unlabeled (145 people). People's responses to open-ended questions were grouped according to their dominant function, and we then looked for themes and patterns in those groups. Mention of independent learning, learning alone, self-directed learning, or making one's own choices formed a theme for each of the four introverted groups: introverted intuitive, introverted sensing, introverted thinking, and introverted feeling. This same cluster of responses appeared as an important theme in the responses of the people who had extraverted intuition as a dominant type, but not for the other extraverted types. For example, only six people who had extraverted feeling as a dominant type included any of these concepts in their answers. It is important to note that we did not ask them about self-directed learning but about learning in general. Nor did we especially look for responses related to self-directed learning; the purpose of the study was to investigate psychological type.

Returning to Candy's (1991) four components of self-directed learning—personal autonomy, self-management, learner control, and autodidaxy—psychological type preferences appear to be relevant to each facet. Tremblay and her colleagues studied autodidactic learners and described them in part as intuitives. The introverted types whom I questioned may have been describing personal autonomy, given their emphasis on independence in their responses. To draw inferences from Candy's composite profile, it may be that learner control and self-management call on the attributes of the thinking function. Kreber (1994), for example, found some evidence of a relationship between self-directed learning readiness and extraverted thinking preferences which provides partial support for this claim.

Educators who are engaged in self-directed learning about their practice or who are working to become more self-directed in their professional development activities need to consider and work with their personal characteristics and preferences. It may not always be the case that a person has a natural preference for control, self-management, autonomy, or independence. If we assume that these are goals of development for educators and the ideal way to develop, some people will have to deliberately foster these processes. Strategies such as those discussed in Chapter Three can be applied to this end.

Critical Reflection and Psychological Type

Jung ([1921] 1971, p. 459) writes: "Thinking and feeling are rational functions in so far as they are decisively influenced by *reflection*. They function most perfectly when they are in the fullest possible accord with the laws of reason." As I discussed in Chapter Four, critical reflection is most commonly defined as a rational, logical, and analytical process. Dictionary definitions of *reflection* include the word *thinking* as a synonym. As Mezirow (1991) describes this core component of transformative learning, critical reflection falls primarily into the domain of the thinking function.

Dissatisfied with this approach, some researchers have attempted to expand the notion of reflection. Mott (1994), for example, analyzed twelve educators' perceptions of intuition in reflective practice. She concludes that intuition has a clear place in reflection and describes three distinct roles it plays: presenting and synthesizing perceptions, guiding practice, and enhancing competence. Schön's emphasis (1983, 1987) on the role of "intuitive knowing" in reflective practice provides a theoretical model for this type of approach.

In practical guides for educators, reflection often incorporates the characteristics of all the psychological type functions. For example, Heimlich and Norland (1994) include a wide variety of topics under the heading "Reflecting on the Teaching and Learning Exchange." In presenting a reflection exercise, they write: "Close your eyes for a moment and imagine what you might hear, see, smell, and feel in a setting that reminded you of your early school days. What images come to mind?" (p. 96). This activity requires the use of the sensing and the intuitive functions. They then advise: "When thinking about the physical environment of the teaching-learning setting, keep in mind these principles" (p. 97). Thus the thinking function is called upon to order the perceptions. Although they do not articulate it, the authors obviously sense the limitations of reflection as it is defined and broaden their use of the concept.

Boyd and Myers (1988), writing from a Jungian perspective, get around this difficulty by saying that *discernment* rather than critical reflection is the means to transformative learning. Discernment is described as an inner journey and a dialogue with the unconscious. A person must be receptive to information from the unconscious, acknowledge its relevance, and allow the disintegration of prior ways of knowing. Working with the unconscious may be as difficult for a person with a preference for the sensing function as reflection is for the person with a preference for intuition.

Such new ways of understanding critical reflection have the potential for illuminating transformative learning. However, it is beyond the scope of this discussion to expand or revise transformative learning theory; rather, it is my intent to apply Mezirow's conceptualization (1991) to educator development. To that end, it is useful to note that the central process, critical reflection, may take quite different forms for people with varying psychological preferences. Although critical reflection and reflective practice are advocated widely and strategies for fostering them are provided (for example, Brookfield, 1987; Mezirow and Associates, 1990; Schön, 1991), surprisingly little has been written about how individuals vary in their aptitudes or preferences for these processes.

Developing critically reflective capacities is often seen to be indicative of a higher level of maturity or consciousness (see Daloz, 1986, for one discussion of this). However, this is not too helpful in attempting to understand individual differences, as all people are described as having the same goal—becoming more mature, conscious, or developed. King and Kitchener's research on reflective judgment (1994) is similar in its basic stance, that people increase their reflective judgment with age and education, and there are some preliminary findings regarding gender differences which the authors advise us to treat with caution. Other individual differences are not addressed.

Kreber (1994) found some evidence of a negative relationship between scores on extraverted thinking and critical thinking, but Watson and Glaser's (1980) assessment of critical thinking was used. Their concept is fundamentally different from critical reflection as I am using the term. We found a positive relationship in a recent survey (Cranton and Knoop, 1995b): as a part of a larger study, people were asked whether they questioned what they read, if they liked solving problems, if they had a critical attitude toward new information, and if they wanted to know the basis of new ideas. Responses to these questions were significantly correlated with extraverted thinking scores and also with extraverted intuitive and introverted thinking scores. Scores on extraverted feeling were negatively correlated, but not strongly so, with the responses to the critical thinking questions.

In Chapter Four, I discussed critical reflection on educator practice as including the articulation of assumptions, the determination of the sources and consequences of those assumptions, critical questioning of assumptions and beliefs about practice, and imagining alternative perspectives on practice. Articulating and questioning assumptions falls within the domain of the thinking function, imagining alternatives within the capabilities of the intuitive function. Educators with these preferences are likely to be more naturally inclined to engage in critical reflection than their colleagues who prefer the feeling or the sensing function. Also, an intuitive person who does not have a strong thinking function would, theoretically, find the articulation and questioning of assumptions a foreign process, though imagination might be his or her forte.

Critical reflection has been presented as an ideal and a goal in the literature. It is something we all should do, and it comes with maturity and increased education. Brookfield (1987, p. 39) points out that this conception is "culturally bound" and "prescriptive" (p. 40), although he does not see these points as invalidating the importance of the process. What also needs to be acknowledged is that critical reflection is easier for some people to do than it is for others. Indeed, the process leading to the transformation of meaning perspectives may not be critical reflection for all individuals.

Educators who are working to develop their practice need to consider whether reflection is natural for them, and if not, what the equivalent process might be. Is it discernment, as Boyd and Myers (1988) propose? Or is it a matter of being "mindful"—"paying attention not only to what is going on around us, but also within us," as Tremmel (1993, p. 447) suggests? Discernment, a dialogue with the unconscious, is an intuitive process; mindfulness, paying attention to the present, is a sensing function process. Individuals with a preference for the feeling function judge, as do thinking types, but by using values rather than logic.

Transformation and Psychological Type

When critical reflection leads to a revision in meaning schemes or perspectives, and when a person acts on the changed view, transformative learning has taken place. As I have suggested, critical reflection may be a different process for some individuals. Nevertheless, everyone has the capacity for transformative learning regardless of the route taken to change. Whenever I have asked a group of educators to describe a major change in their perspectives on practice using a critical incident or life story exercise, almost without exception people have had stories to tell. The details and circumstances vary dramatically, but people do change their meaning perspectives.

To date, there have been no published investigations of the relationships between preferences for psychological types and the nature of the transformative learning process. It is hoped that discussions such as the one presented here will excite the imagination of researchers. Elsewhere, I propose a matrix of type preferences by aspects of transformative learning (Cranton, 1994a, p. 108) and present a theoretical rationale for my predictions. Several components of this matrix refer to critical reflection, discussed in the previous section. Here, I first point out a few discrepancies between Jung's and Mezirow's theories and then summarize my views on how educators who have different psychological type preferences might revise their meaning schemes and perspectives.

Although there are other conceptualizations, as mentioned earlier, Mezirow (1991) describes transformative learning as essentially a rational process. He writes that "[t]hinking and learning are overlapping terms" (p. 12). He defines learning as "using thought processes to make or revise an interpretation in a new context, applying the knowledge resulting from prior thought and/or prior tacit learning to construe meaning in a new encounter" (p. 13). Mezirow sees "[p]erception or prereflective learning . . . [as occurring] prior to the use of language to form categories" (p. 15). To give one final definition central to the theory, rationality is described as "a process of assessing the reasons and justification for a meaning scheme. This may involve a review of empirical evidence or a best judgment made through an informed consensus" (p. 31). In other words, following this theoretical perspective, learning takes place through thinking, and both are rational.

According to Jung's typology, thinking is but one of four functions that people use. His definition of thinking—"the psychological function which, following its own laws, brings the contents of ideation into conceptual connection with one another" (p. 481)— is similar to Mezirow's definition. Jung also sees thinking as being only one form of rationality, the other being feeling, in which judgments are made based on values or a simple acceptance or rejection. Finally, Jung describes perception (or irrationality) as being "beyond reason" (p. 454), rather than "prereflective" as does Mezirow. Jung (p. 455) sees the irrational as never being the object of science but "of the greatest importance for a practical psychology." The perceptive functions, sensing and intuition, "lack all rational direction" (p. 455) but are not "unreasonable" (p. 371). Jung is quite clear that perceptive and rational functions are equally valid and that each has advantages over the other, although the two kinds of people will have trouble understanding each other's preferences.

Suggestions for Transformation by Type

Working with the differences between Mezirow's and Jung's perspectives on learning and individual differences, I suggest how educators with each type preference might engage in transformative learning. It is important to remember here that no person is a pure type; consequently, the following suggestions apply to a person only to the extent that he or she has a preference for that way of being.

Extraverted Thinking

Transformative learning theory seems to be written about people with a preference for extraverted thinking. Questioning assumptions, engaging in critical reflection, and participating in rational discourse are all natural expressions of the thinking function. However, when it comes to the product of the process, the revision of meaning schemes or perspectives, individuals who are strongly inclined toward extraverted thinking may not be as likely to undergo that change as are others. They often use reasoning and logical analysis. As a result, they have developed, in adulthood, strong principles, convictions, and assumptions that are not easily shaken.

Extraverted Feeling

The extraverted feeling function does not engage easily in critical reflection, as described in transformative learning theory. Individuals who have this preference base their judgments on values and general feelings of like-dislike or acceptance-rejection. On the other hand, they like to be in harmony with the values of other individuals around them and with the values of the society they live in. When it comes to the revision of meaning schemes and perspectives, they will easily adapt—change their perspectives. To people who do not share this preference, use of the extraverted feeling function may appear to be shallow or superficial, a giving up of beliefs. However, for people whose nature this is, it is a genuine change and often a profound learning experience.

Extraverted Sensing

A preference for extraverted sensing means that the person is interested in objects, events, and facts, without consideration of the assumptions underlying their perceptions. Consequently, most aspects of transformative learning as described by Mezirow are foreign to this person. When it comes to a revision of a meaning scheme or perspective, extraverted sensing types would need to be surrounded by or immersed in a series of sensations of a nature that is different from their past experience. A change in culture, career, or personal circumstance could lead to a change in perspective. This would not take place through reflection but rather as a product of the new sensations.

Extraverted Intuitive

In an earlier work, I described people with this preference as being aware of their values and assumptions and open to questioning them, but reluctant to revise them (Cranton, 1994a). However, discussions with extraverted intuitive types in my current research have led me to question these assumptions. These individuals see themselves as being "slaves of their visions," and they have difficulty relating to terms such as perspectives, assumptions, beliefs, or values. It could be that they are unaware of their meaning perspectives, but it could also mean that the process of transformation is different for them. Perhaps they will revise a meaning perspective only when a new vision leads them to see the world in a different way. This is not, of course, in line with Mezirow's definition of meaning perspectives, but Mezirow sees transformative learning as a rational process, and the extraverted intuitive function is not rational. Interesting research questions can be addressed in this area.

Introverted Thinking

People with a preference for the introverted thinking function are "strongly influenced by ideas though [their] ideas have their origin not in objective data but in . . . subjective foundation" (Jung, [1921] 1971, p. 383). An inclination toward introversion means that the person is more interested in inward (subjective) processes. Rational thought, reasoning, questioning, and especially engaging in reflection are preferences of this type of person, and these are processes that can lead to transformative learning. However, as is the case for extraverted thinking types, introverted individuals do not like to give up their ideas. It is with reluctance that they will revise their assumptions or perspectives. Rather than an external stimulus, it is likely to be a flaw in reasoning, discovered by reflection, that will lead to change through introverted thinking.

Introverted Feeling

Similar to their extraverted feeling counterparts, people with a preference for introverted feeling have an inclination to want to maintain harmony in their world. Their judgments are made based on a subjective or personal interpretation of the world, meaning that the process is somewhat different for them. They may agree with others to avoid conflict or controversy, but when the judgment is subjectified, an actual change in perspective may not take place. Transformative learning would likely be an intense inner upheaval for introverted feeling types rather than the easygoing adjustment that extraverted individuals make in order to stay congruent with their surroundings.

Introverted Sensing

When the introverted sensing function is dominant, the person reacts to stimuli from the external world but "alters the sense-perception at its source, thus depriving it of the character of a purely objective influence" (Jung, [1921] 1971, p. 394). The individual is sensitive to events, objects, and people but attaches a personal meaning to them. It is difficult to say, then, when an experience or what kind of experience would lead to revised meaning schemes or perspectives; this would depend on the way that person interpreted the experience. It could be that through the subjectification process, the introverted sensing type reconciles discrepancies (simply changes the experience into what he or she wants it to be) and therefore does not easily transform.

Introverted Intuitive

When introverted intuition is dominant for a person, the hunches and images come from within, from the unconscious. Boyd and Myers' description (1988) of discernment as a dialogue with the unconscious seems to describe best what this person would go through in transformational learning. As I mentioned earlier, it is with the intuitive function that there is the most difficulty in reconciling Mezirow's learning process (1991) with Jung's descriptions of preferences. When the subjectification of the introverted attitude is looked at in conjunction with the irrational nature of intuition, it becomes hard to see how meaning schemes and perspectives would be revised. The introverted intuitives with whom I discussed this issue in my current research could not identify with the concepts.

Research is needed on the experiences of individuals with different preferences and characteristics going through transformative learning. When educators change their theory of practice or make revisions to their philosophy of education, what takes place? For some this may be a rational process stimulated by reading, discussions with others, or thoughtful analysis of what they do. Others may adapt their practice to fit in with the culture of the organization for which they work. Some educators may only revise their views of practice when they have the opportunity to experience different approaches. Others may change their vision of being an educator as a side effect of pursuing a larger improvement plan. However individual educators go about revising their perspectives on practice, it is a major and sometimes difficult transition. An illustration may be helpful in understanding the process.

Transformation and Psychological Type: An Illustration

Fiametta teaches basic literacy skills to immigrant adults. The composition of her groups varies, but she usually has a majority of Asian students. The groups are small, no more than twenty in each, and most have a goal of wanting to enter or continue with higher education, for which they need stronger English language skills.

Her psychological type profile shows Fiametta to have a strong preference for extraverted intuition and a secondary preference for extraverted feeling. On the extraverted-introverted continuum, Fiametta is clearly extraverted, though she has a slight inclination toward introverted feeling.

Fiametta has always loved teaching. She has worked in her current position without any lessening of her enthusiasm for eighteen years. She explains that "the people are always different, so it never gets boring." When asked what it is about teaching that appeals to her so strongly, Fiametta explains that she can "make such a difference to people" and that it is "so wonderful to see them learn and get more comfortable with the language and make such dramatic changes." Fiametta speaks proudly of some of her students' having gone on to graduate studies while others have become community leaders.

When I first asked Fiametta to talk about any major changes she had made in her perspectives on her practice, she felt that none had occurred. "I have always loved teaching and I have always been a good teacher," she said. The notion of having assumptions about her practice was also not something to which Fiametta could relate. She told me, "I do not really think about what I do, ever. I just know what to do at any moment and I do it and I feel that it is right or it works or it doesn't, and if it doesn't I immediately change what I'm doing, without any concrete thinking about it. I don't ever assume something will work; I can't see that I have assumptions about teaching."

I had several such conversations with Fiametta as she and I tried to understand how extraverted intuitive educators might experience transformative development. We had eliminated the use of the words *meaning perspective, meaning scheme, assumptions, beliefs,* and *values* in our discussion. Fiametta said, "I remember a few years ago when my whole vision of the role of education in society changed. Would that be related to what we're talking about? I didn't actually change my practice, I mean I didn't do anything differently, but I did change the way I saw things."

Fiametta had viewed her role as an educator as including not only working with language skills but helping individuals to assimilate into the North American culture. She took them to movies and restaurants and discussed differences in dress and body language. Her goal was to "make them into little Canadians," as she revealingly described it in retrospect. The change that she experienced was one in which she came to see that her students valued their own culture, and that she was not valuing them as people when she tried to take away their cultural values. But Fiametta did not recall ever questioning her views or reflecting on her role as she said, "I suppose I must have done so." Instead, she felt that it was a sudden change, "a whole new thing, just there suddenly, and why hadn't I seen that before, that I was belittling them, not in what I did but in my mind."

Summary

An interest in differences among individuals has been a part of our understanding of education for many decades, since educational researchers moved away from general methods-comparisons studies in the mid-1950s. On the other hand, not much has come of the empirical efforts to relate individual characteristics to learning success. When we look at educators as learners and how educators develop, we know even less about the nature of individual differences in that process.

I have used Jung's theory of psychological type as a way to discuss how educators might vary on their approaches to their professional development. I chose psychological type theory as it maintains a subjective as well as an objective understanding of human beings and does not minimize the complexity of human character.

There is some research evidence that people with a preference for the intuitive psychological type are more likely to be or to become self-directed learners. If a more complex model of self-directed learning is used, such as Candy's four dimensions (1991), this relationship may not be as straightforward as is indicated by the empirical research.

Critical reflection, the central process in transformative development, appears to be the domain of those educators with a preference for the thinking function. The concept of reflection has troubled some researchers, and alternative views of the process have been proposed. It may be that people with different natures experience this part of their development in varying ways.

According to Mezirow (1991), when transformative learning has taken place people revise their meaning schemes or meaning perspectives. All people have the capacity to transform, and most people do change their perspective or frame of reference at some points in their lives. The way they go through this is likely to be dependent on their character and their preferences.

Finally, I have presented an illustration of an educator who has a preference for intuition. I described her difficulty with articulating assumptions and her understanding of transformative development.

Chapter Seven

Transformative Development in Work and Social Contexts

Educators are change agents. We work with learners to foster their growth and development. We are models and mentors in our workplaces. We promote change within our profession. We are often active in our communities and in the larger society in which we live. On many levels, change and reform are the responsibility of adult educators. Once we master the technical skills of teaching and go on to develop our philosophies of practice, we develop an interest in the broader context of educational practice. Self-directed learning about our practice, critical reflection on our work, and our own transformative development lead us naturally into the role of change agent. We question policies that are obstacles in our work, we challenge the views of our colleagues, we use our skills to initiate activist groups in the community.

Adult education has its roots in social reform. In the 1800s, adult educators were seen to be radicals or reformers, depending on one's perspective (for example, see Selman, 1989). Working primarily in literacy education, they were working against the status quo by helping people free themselves from the constraint of not being able to read. In more modern times, we think of Freire's work (1970) in this regard, especially his concept of conscientization, whereby adults "achieve a deepening awareness of both the sociocultural reality which shapes their lives and . . . their capacity to transform that reality through action upon it" (p. 27).

Transformative learning theory is grounded in part in Habermas's conceptualization of human interests and knowledge and of communicative action (1971, 1984). Our practical interests lead us to want to understand each other and the norms of our society. Our emancipatory interests lead us to critically question perceived constraints and to work toward self-awareness. Welton (1993) summarizes Habermas's contribution to adult education. Among other points, he argues that Habermas's work "challenges adult educators to consider why we have been blind to the ways in which institutions enable or constrain our capacity to learn to be the kind of persons we most want to be" (p. 89) and "encourages us to ask whether our institutions, large and small, truly enable human beings to unfold their potentials (cognitive, moral, technical, aesthetic) in their daily routine interactions" (p. 89).

Although Mezirow has been criticized for not emphasizing social action in his work (Collard and Law, 1989), transformative learning is by definition concerned with social change. When individuals have the choice of seeing the world in a different way and when they are able to question the sources of their beliefs, this is the beginning of social change. When people are limited by their perspectives, change will not take place. Of course, social systems gather their own power in a way that makes them inaccessible to questioning (Habermas, 1984)—who questions what "they" say in the legal system or the mass communications system?—but it is not until people see themselves as having the power of questioning systems that social reform can occur. Individuals come to know themselves by becoming conscious of the sources of their perspectives. When this awareness exists, people are then able to negotiate social change.

Educators may be agents of change, or alternatively, keepers of the status quo. The socialization of teachers, defined as the process by which they are inducted into the educational system, works against the reformer role. Kincheloe (1991, p. 12) argues that the preparation of teachers has "emphasized the technique of teaching, focusing on the inculcation of the 'best' method to deliver a body of predetermined facts and the familiarization of teachers with the 'proper' format for lesson plans which enhances supervision efficiency and thus allows for stricter accountability." He is writing about the training of certified public school teachers; to some extent adult educators escape this process as no preparatory training is usually required of them. On the other hand, Kincheloe's description also encompasses much of what we regard as professional development for adult educators.

When educators are critically reflective and engaged in inquiry about their practice, Kincheloe (1991, p. 16) writes, then this "perspective cannot view the educational act separately from a social vision, i.e., a view of a desirable future." Critical teachers "cannot avoid the political role of promoting critical self-reflection in the society" (p. 23). Educators' individual development and their role in work and social contexts cannot be separated. Learning is both a process of socialization and a process of change. Jarvis (1992b, p. 24) describes this as a paradox: "learning is both at the heart of all social conformity and also at the heart of all social change. Without the ability to learn, there would be no society and no humanity. But paradoxically, it is learning that also helps generate some forms of change."

It is my contention here that the educator who engages in self-directed, reflective, and potentially transformative learning will be likely to promote the same among his or her learners and hence will be an agent of social change. In his interpretation of Habermas, Held (1980, p. 256) describes this dualism well: "The process of emancipation, then, entails the transcendence of such systems of distorted communication. This process, in turn, requires engaging in critical reflection and criticism. It is only through reflection that domination, in its many forms, can be unmasked." The educator involved in the process of emancipation will necessarily work with that process throughout his or her practice.

I use the term *social* as a broad descriptor, pertaining to our interactions with others in the workplace, the community, and society. It is not my intent to address here the constructs of race, gender, and class in the literature on critical social theory, but rather to discuss how the individual educator can work toward change within the context of his or her practice. In this chapter, I work from the more narrow to the more general social worlds of the educator. I discuss educators' roles in social change in their organizations and institutions, in the profession of educators, and in the society in which they live and work. I propose that these roles are different for people who have varying psychological preferences. Finally, I discuss the advocation of change in work and social contexts as a goal of educators' development.

Working in Organizations and Institutions

Educators have many and varied opportunities to act as agents of change within their own organizations and institutions, whether these be in formal or informal roles. For human resource developers, for example, this work may be a part of their formal role, but for others it may be a matter of acting as a model, of offering support and advice to colleagues, or of engaging in conversations with others in the workplace. Organizational change and development take many forms, from interpersonal approaches to systemwide endeavors (Cummings and Huse, 1989). Educators can participate in existing strategies or initiate development in their workplace.

Jarvis (1992b) describes the modern world of work as technological and bureaucratic. Individuals "learn to become divided selves and to cope with life" (p. 180); "[l]earning how to fit in is a nonreflective learning process" (p. 180). Often formal learning in the workplace is "institutionally sponsored, classroom-based and highly structured" (Marsick and Watkins, 1990, p. 12). Kincheloe's assessment of organizations and institutions (1991) is even more devastating. He describes existing programs, such as the Quality of Working Life movement, as "particularly dangerous because they have given the public the impression that workers are full participants in management decision making" (p. 11). He proposes that workers are given autonomy to make insignificant decisions so that they will be less inclined to want to participate in larger decisions related to production or collective bargaining. Teachers are no exception; he argues that teachers are increasingly deskilled through the imposition of mandatory curriculum and other restrictive policies.

Habermas (1976, pp. 11–12) maintains that such social systems reproduce themselves through production and socialization, social labor, and systems of roles. He sees language as a medium that functions as a kind of transformer. Through the exchange of experiences and perceptions, individuals within a social system can function to change that system.

What kinds of strategies can educators use or what roles might they assume in working toward social change in their organizations and institutions? Gass, Goldman, and Priest (1992) report that American businesses spend $60 billion annually on training, yet we still seem to have bureaucratic, technocratic, and oppressive systems. On the other hand, Watkins and Marsick (1993) present eighteen vignettes of organizational development in which growth, learning, and possibly transformations are taking place. Perhaps if educators turn their energies and use their expertise to question the organization itself, more meaningful change can take place than that described in Kincheloe's (1991) pessimistic summary. I have selected but a few examples of models and approaches that educators interested in social change within their workplace might consider.

Model I and Model II Theories

More than two decades ago, Argyris (1971) described the tasks of organizational development to be generating valid information, creating opportunities for people to make free choices, and creating conditions for internal commitment to these choices. He describes the transition to this kind of workplace as filled with "vacillation, ambiguity, pain, [and] frustration" (p. 156). With Schön (1987), this approach was developed into two models of theories-in-use. Model I uses strategies of control and protection of the self. Model II behavior includes those tasks listed above. Argyris and Schön designed a professional development procedure, using case studies and role playing, to help individuals move from Model I to Model II interactions with others. Schön (1987, p. 264) describes the Model II heuristics: couple advocacy of your position with inquiry into the other's beliefs; state the attribution you are making, tell how you got to it, and ask for the other's confirmation or disconfirmation; and if you experience a dilemma, express it publicly. The potential for transformative learning is clear. The development procedure has been applied in a wide variety of contexts, including higher education (Smith and Schwartz, 1985).

Action Research

Action research is based on the assumption that people are able to take more effective action when they conduct research on their practice together. Individuals interested in understanding their practice or solving a work problem join together, define the situation, collect and analyze relevant data, and develop alternative strategies to try out in the workplace. Kurt Lewin (1946) is credited with the first conceptualization of this approach. Action research has recently gained popularity in higher education (Cross, 1990; Zuber-Skerritt, 1992) and public school education (Kincheloe, 1991; Carr and Kemmis, 1986). The philosophy underlying action research is one of equality and empowerment, with workers and professionals conducting investigations into the nature and outcomes of their own work. This is in contrast to the traditional research model of the expert researcher "studying down" to the practitioner (Kincheloe, 1991, p. 13) and gaining knowledge that is not usually even disseminated to those who contributed. Action research is derived from critical theory and falls into Habermas's (1971) description of using the critical-research paradigm to obtain emancipatory knowledge: knowledge about oneself that leads to freedom from constraints imposed by others.

One example of using action research in the workplace is described in a Scandinavian model presented by Elden and Gjersvik (1994). Two explicit goals are given: to democratize work life publicly, and to have a research process which is in itself democratized. The model comprises five elements (pp. 32–33):

- Purposes and value choice: the selection of problems to study that will contribute to both general knowledge and practical solutions
- Contextual focus: dealing with real-life problems in a practical way so as to conduct interdisciplinary and practice-theory rather than theory-practice investigations
- Change-based data and sense making: the collection of data over time so as to interpret the consequences of change and make sense from the results
- Participation in the research process: the involvement of those who experience the real-world problem in the search for solutions
- Knowledge diffusion: spreading a solution to the chosen problem to others and specifying learning outcomes

In a recent research methods course, I worked with a group to explore the three research paradigms: empirical-analytical, interpretive, and critical. In his journal, one participant, a science teacher, wrote, "I never thought of research as something that teachers could do or be involved in, I always thought of it as something that experts did and something that did not have much relevance to my day-to-day life. I am still struggling with the notion that I, an ordinary teacher, can actually do research. All teachers should learn something about this kind of research. My colleagues think of research as too complex to understand, not that we talk about research very much, but I know that is what they think."

Educators working in any environment—business, industry, community groups, hospitals, or educational institutions—can initiate and participate in action research projects. When people have the power to learn about their own practice through research rather than be subjects in others' research, social change within the workplace can be fostered.

Feminist Pedagogy

Unlike the previous two approaches I have described, feminist pedagogy is relatively new. It has its source in the women's movement of the 1960s and 1970s and has gained popularity with the growth of women's studies programs and research. Although there is considerable variation among the models and philosophies discussed in the literature, there appear to be some common themes. Feminist pedagogy is concerned with (1) providing learning experiences that lead to change in learners' lives, (2) an emphasis on relationships and connections rather than separation and competition, and (3) individuals' personal power (Maher, 1987; Tisdell, 1993).

Tisdell (1993, pp. 101–102) describes the implications of feminist pedagogy for the practical realm of adult education:

- Educators should consider how their curriculum challenges the nature of structured power relations based on gender, race, and class.
- Educators should develop and experiment with teaching strategies that prove to be emancipatory.
- Courses should be developed that deal directly with power relations based on gender, race, and class.

- Educators should attempt to address the way their own unconscious behavior in the learning environment either challenges or reproduces power distributions.

Similarly, but following a more general model, Hart (1990) lists the main principles of consciousness raising and their implications for educational practice:

- Oppression has to be acknowledged by the educator and the learner.
- Personal experience needs to be critically reflected upon, and some ways of knowing may have to be undone.
- Only a learning group that is relatively homogeneous with respect to major social differences would share an interest in liberation and similar experiences.
- A structure of equality must exist among all participants, including the educator.
- A certain theoretical distance should be maintained so as not to have the validation of personal feelings as the only goal.
- Each group will go through phases or stages in its development, moving from surface issues through deeper and more painful issues and then outward toward possibilities for the future.

By now, the feminist literature has led to a common understanding of women as having a different voice or a different way of knowing (Belenky, Clinchy, Goldberger, and Tarule, 1986). Educators who are working toward social change in the workplace can incorporate these understandings into their practice. Clark, Caffarella, and Ingram (1994) found, for example, in a study of twenty-five midmanagement women that

- Women prefer collaborative and participatory leadership styles in which relationships play a central role.
- Career development paths for women have a nonlinear pattern.
- Intimacy issues, such as balancing professional and personal lives, and identity issues, such as developing an authentic way of leading, are of ongoing importance to women.

A brief look at feminist pedagogy tells us that the philosophies underlying practice and the strategies advocated in this literature are relevant to social change in our organizations and institutions.

Working Within the Community of Educators

It is easy enough for practicing educators, writers, researchers, and theorists to fall into a rather comfortable accommodation to current trends and ideas, thereby abandoning the critical practice of adult education. As teachers become deskilled through socialization, the imposition of policy, and the nature of their training (Kincheloe, 1991), so too can adult educators become decontextualized and depoliticized (Griffin, 1987) and supportive of social conformity (Collins, 1988). The research and writing on self-directed learning following from Malcolm Knowles's work provide one such example. Brookfield (1993, p. 227) writes: "We have so many people working on self-directed learning that their numbers support a Commission of Professors of Adult Education task force on this topic, and an annual international symposium devoted solely to research and theory in the area." Collins (1994) describes his concern with the reification of self-directed learning and the resultant deployment of the concept as technique.

As with any profession, to stay the same and to follow in the footsteps of those who precede us is easier than to critically question our colleagues and consequently our own practice. Adult educators who have social change as a goal of their practice may also view that goal in relation to their own profession. How can we do this? Collins (1994, p. 101) writes that "we need to maintain ongoing critique, and to identify sensible strategies for resistance against repressive curriculum formats which are sustained through dubious professionalizing agendas." Perhaps we can avoid reaching Kincheloe's (1991) description of the public education system by resisting such professionalizing agendas in adult education.

As I discussed in Chapter Six, people with a preference for the intuitive function are likely to be those who are interested in social change; conversely, people with a preference for the sensing function are likely to be those interested in practical or "sensible strategies" (Collins, 1994, p. 101). The stronger the preference for intuition, the less the preference for sensing, says Jung ([1921]

1971), as these are opposing ways of perceiving the world. But we have to devise practical strategies for change and development. The recent literature contains some promising notions regarding working together to challenge our assumptions about practice and to develop as educators.

Professionalization and Professional Associations

From one perspective, professionalization, whether formal or informal, can be in conflict with transformative development among educators. To the extent that we stop thinking critically and simply follow traditional policies or adopt the espoused theories of our profession, this will be the case. On the other hand, if critical questioning becomes a way of viewing ourselves as professionals, this can work to our advantage. As Spikes (1989, p. 64) points out, adult educators have a "rich history of banding together at the local, regional, and national levels to form groups, councils, and associations that serve specific or more general needs of the field." We need to be conscious, however, of what the goals of these associations are or become over time.

Using Foucault's framework for discourse analysis (1972), Wilson (1993) investigated the content of the seven editions of handbooks published between 1934 and 1989 by the American Association of Adult Education, the Adult Education Association, and the American Association for Adult and Continuing Education. The early handbooks were a compilation of descriptions of various components of the field, through a listing of program and institutional examples. Very quickly, though, the handbooks became a catalogue of scientific studies of adult education practice with a goal of improving practice. Wilson uses Habermas's framework of kinds of knowledge (1971), and the research paradigms used to obtain knowledge, to identify the handbooks as following an empirical-analytic paradigm. The function of empirical research is to learn to control. Wilson (1993, p. 12) writes: "The handbooks represent just how systematic and pervasive this drive and its intellectual underpinnings have been" and, further, that "the handbooks demonstrate very clearly how scientific knowledge has been used to define the field and thus control the development of professionalization."

Zuber-Skerritt (1992, p. 118) writes about educators in higher education, but her comments are relevant to all adult educators. She argues that educators should participate in decisions about the context within which they work, and "instead of leaving these decisions and the formulation of their educational, theoretical framework to outside experts and educational researchers, they can be active participants in the process; and they will be changed in this process from uncritical technocrats to critical and self-critical action researchers into teaching and student learning. . . ." Regardless of whether it is through action research, as Zuber-Skerritt proposes, or through other means, educators can use their professional associations, both formal and informal, to advocate a critical approach to practice.

Some strategies to work toward this goal might be

- To take leadership positions in professional associations, as suggested by Shelton and Spikes (1991), and advocate critical questioning of our practice
- To engage in action research, as proposed by Zuber-Skerritt (1992), to understand adult education practice and disseminate this work to colleagues through professional meetings
- To participate in professional associations, contribute to their newsletters or journals, and write letters and reviews to challenge the unquestioned views
- To form one's own professional association or start a newsletter in an area where none exists and encourage critical questioning within that group
- To be conscious of the process of professionalization and where the boundary between socialization and professionalization exists—question when things seem questionable
- To look critically at all statements about how things are "always" done in the profession and question people and organizations who issue such statements
- To deliberately and consciously interact with colleagues, raising issues related to professionalization and to critical practice

Collaborative Inquiry

In his theory of communicative competence, Habermas (1984) argues that all speech is oriented to the idea of genuine consensus. Critical theory is grounded in a normative standard that is inherent in the structure of social action and language. This notion, which is essentially one of the democratization of knowledge, has long been at the heart of practice in adult education. Equally important, and not contradictory as it first seems, is the notion of individualism. In practice, individualism has been termed self-direction and contains the belief that people should make their own decisions about their learning. Brookfield (1993, p. 231–232) says it best when he writes that

> by attending to the oppositional elements embedded in these ideas, we are able to create some important strategic openings for building critical practice in the field. If issues of power and control are seen as central to an analysis of individualism, and if discussions of self-direction focus on the need for people to be responsible for framing their own choices and making their own decisions rather than ceding these responsibilities to others, then programs which espouse self-direction will have to address the politically contentious questions of voice, relevance and authority. Moreover, these questions will be seen to spring from what most Americans would consider to be an appropriate concern with issues of democratic control.

Collaborative inquiry is a recent phenomenon in the literature, but it is one that has a long history. Perhaps through a revival of this philosophy and especially its application in practice, educators can work toward social change within their professional community. The Group for Collaborative Inquiry (1993, p. 43) points out that "even in a field such as adult education which has historically concerned itself with the project of universal democracy and the related problems of inclusion, institutions and policies are minimally influenced by the knowledge these constituencies themselves have." They argue that as a result, there is a preference in the field for the knowledge of scholars, knowledge born of reason and science, or in other words, instrumental knowledge. The Group for Collaborative Inquiry suggests that knowledge produced in adult education must be inclusive—it must include different ways of knowing, different sources of knowledge, and different modes of expression. They make several practical suggestions for change within the community of educators (pp. 49–50):

- We must create different structures for judging what is good in our field.
- We should question and reconstruct processes for nominating office holders and assessing manuscripts for publication.
- We need to examine our processes for coaching and mentoring new colleagues.
- We must strive toward raising personal consciousness about the ways in which we exclude others.

As important as these suggestions are, it may well be the process of collaborative inquiry itself that is the key to change in our community. Kincheloe (1991, pp. 20–21) argues that the sharing of knowledge and research skills, especially with the disempowered, "negates the cult of the expert. It helps destroy the myth that men and women should seek guidance from those blessed with society's credentials to direct them. In this way it celebrates human self-direction." He also points out that under such a model, the practitioner becomes an active political agent and views education as "a vehicle to build an egalitarian community" (p. 21).

Another collaborative group (thINQ, 1994) emphasizes their five distinctive voices and individual reflection as well as the group process. Collaborative inquiry does not minimize the role of the individual but rather should serve to enhance it as people gain power through equal participation in a process. Within our community of adult educators, collaboration can lead to a questioning and challenging of professional practice that may not be possible through other avenues.

Educators might consider the use of electronic networks as an alternative to face-to-face collaborative work. Many adult educators are isolated—the only one in the field in their organization or institution, or practicing in small or remote locations. Even for educators who are members of a department or group, obtaining fresh perspectives from other areas is always a priority. The potential of the Internet for the formation of collaborative groups and discussion forums is clear.

Working in Our Society

We often read that social reform is a goal of adult education; some of us follow the debates about which comes first, social change or individual change. However, when as a part of a larger study I asked 745 people (approximately one-half of whom were educators) to indicate their agreement with the statement "A goal of teaching is social reform," the average rating was on the negative or disagreement side of the scale (Cranton and Knoop, 1995c). When I looked at educators as a separate sample, the average rating was still negative.

One reason for this incongruence between the literature and people's perspectives may be, as Boshier (1994) points out, that there is no map of what adult education is. He defines four paradigms: (1) functionalism, with a concern for social order and social integration; (2) interpretivism, with a concern for understanding individuals' subjective meanings of the world; (3) radical humanism, with an interest in overthrowing or transcending existing social arrangements; and (4) radical structuralism, with a commitment to the overthrow of social structures that are distorted or false. If people interpret adult education in these, and probably other, divergent ways, then one could not expect to find general agreement with a statement that social reform is a goal.

Boshier (1994, p. 43) describes adult education as "pluralistic" and implies that people holding these different views should be able to coexist peacefully. This notion could be taken further. The argument could be made that despite the language people use to describe their perception of the goals of adult education, social change in some form is at the core of our practice. If an educator is working with the technical skills required to use a computer, the basic skills required to obtain a high school certificate, the living skills required to deal with an abusive upbringing, or the practical skills required to give a better presentation, the learners are gaining alternatives and the freedom to choose between alternatives. This is the essence of change.

Brookfield (1987, p. 57) points out that "critical thinkers make explicit the connections between the personal and political in their lives. They are aware that individual crises often reflect wider social changes." He implies that individual concerns and social concerns are inseparable. If a person is a victim of a violent crime, knows that the crime rate in her city or country is high, and is aware of proposed gun legislation in the country, the issues are fused. Sometimes collective action is needed to deal with individual problems, and sometimes individual issues lead people to work toward social reform. Brookfield (1987, p. 58) gives the example of the spread of AIDS as a situation in which "the most private of tragedies has become an activator of collective action."

"For a critical perspective on adult education the initial task is to identify social structures and practices which (mis)shape social learning processes and undermine capacities adults already possess to control their own education" (Collins, 1994, p. 100). How can the adult educator who has social change as an explicit goal in his or her theory of practice work toward that goal?

- As is suggested in most of the literature, we need to be conscious of our own beliefs, values, and assumptions regarding social change. This involves keeping informed of current issues, reflecting on our own assumptions, discussing issues with others, and questioning ourselves and others.
- We need to engage in political learning, "questioning the basis on which individuals, groups, and systems exercise . . . powers over one's life" (Brookfield, 1987, p. 165).
- We can ask "awkward" questions of our organizations, systems, and governments—why the managers are predominantly white males, why the cleaning staff is predominantly Hispanic.
- We can learn about and become involved in political movements: environmentalist groups, gun legislation lobbies, peace movements, issues for which we feel a strong interest and commitment.
- We can initiate activist groups, discussion groups, or study circles related to issues we feel strongly about.
- We need to learn to read images critically and to question the values portrayed in the media and in advertising, as suggested by Kellner (1991) among others.
- We can engage in small acts as well as larger commitments: teaching another person how to read, or volunteering some time to a women's shelter.
- We can write about social issues in local newspapers, newsletters, or professional journals.
- We can speak about social issues in the community, in our organization or institution, at conferences, or in invited talks and addresses.

These are but some examples of what we can do. The ways in which educators choose to promote change depend on their interests and their nature, as I discuss later in this chapter. Each of the actions or strategies suggested above has as its focus critical questioning, critical thinking, and the opening up of alternative ways of seeing our society both for ourselves and others. At this time, it is also worthwhile to consider Jarvis's paradox (1992b). He points out that the assumption underlying adult education practice is that individuals are free to pursue their own interests and that such an approach is a "weak form of liberalism" (p. 223). He argues that if "everyone were to engage in [learning] in a reflective and critical manner all the time, the basis of society would be undermined" and that if "everybody were reflective, innovative learners, society would need the state . . . to create stability and unity" (p. 223). Consequently, we have critical thinking both sustaining democracy, as Brookfield (1987) presents it, and critical thinking as threatening the procedures that allow the state to function smoothly.

Just as the balance between individualism and collaboration is essential to social well-being, so is the balance between critical thinking and the social system. The seeming contradiction between these two forces and how we deal with this paradox in our practice needs to be a part of the consciousness of educators who are working toward change in social contexts.

Individual Differences in Approaches to Change

In Chapter Six, I discussed how educators may engage in transformative learning about their practice in different ways as a result of their psychological nature. These individual differences are equally important when we develop our roles as agents of change in our practice. It might be natural and comfortable for one person to initiate a lobby group or join a political movement, but it could be unnatural and difficult for another person to do so.

Active, outgoing involvement in political and social movements may come more easily to educators with a preference for the extraverted intuitive function. The intuitive inclination leads people to imagine how things could be, and the extraverted attitude is focused on the external environment rather than the self. As a part of a larger study, a colleague and I asked 892 people to indicate their agreement or disagreement with the statements "I can bring about major change" and "I can inspire people and bring about their enthusiasm" (Cranton and Knoop, 1995c, p. 9). We found a strong positive relationship between ratings of these questions and people's scores on extraverted intuition.

Educators with a preference for the other extraverted functions may express their roles as change agents in different ways (Knoop, 1995). Use of the thinking function could be demonstrated through being good organizers, public speakers, fund raisers, or planners of events. Extraverted educators who naturally use their sensing function may be able to work on the practical implementation of changes suggested by others; they would also be expected to have a good sense of concrete reality and could be the ones to take over the financial matters for a group or the details of putting on events and functions. People who prefer to use their feeling function may not be as interested in dealing with the conflict and controversy involved in change, but they could enjoy working directly with people in any group during the implementation of change.

We would not expect that educators who are more inclined to introversion would take to the outgoing, action-oriented aspects of promoting social change. They might prefer the equally important background roles in organizing events or activities, working one-on-one with individuals during the implementation of a project, working with small groups in areas such as literacy education, or writing articles, newsletters, pamphlets, or guides.

It is important not to belittle any of the roles that educators with different preferences might play in the change process. The most charismatic public speaker may not be able to organize the event at which she is to speak. The best public relations person may not be able to present ideas convincingly. The educator with the most innovative ideas for change may find that he has no skills for raising funds for his group. The strongest leader of a political movement may be at a loss for words when it comes to talking to the individuals affected by the change. A part of our development as educators involves understanding ourselves and the best ways we can work toward a critical perspective on our practice.

Social Change and Educator Development

Increasing our awareness of how we are agents of change as educators is a vital part of our development. Brookfield (1990a) argues that teaching is inherently political.

I know that across the world in regimes of the right and left teachers who challenge prevailing ways of thinking and acting are being
tortured and murdered by police forces, the military, death squads,
and vigilantes. Some educational institutions in less extreme societies also impose their own constraints on critical questioning, such
as denial of promotion and tenure, inability to get one's work published, progressive isolation within one's institution, or ridicule for
one's supposed eccentricities. So, rather than teaching being the
last refuge of the naive or politically disinterested, it is actually one
of the most intensely politicized occupations one can choose
(Brookfield, 1990a, p. 191).

Beginning educators may not see social change as their role;
indeed, if we accept Boshier's four paradigms of adult education
(1994), a good proportion of people would not describe this as a
part of what they do. New teachers and those with a functionalist
perspective would consider professional development as the acquisition of techniques and strategies for the improvement of their
delivery of the subject matter or the training they provide. I discussed these views in Chapters Two and Three and argued that
there are different kinds of knowledge about educational practice
and therefore different ways of obtaining that knowledge. But also,
seeing oneself as a change agent will not be a part of one's perspective until there is a basic comfort level with the techniques of
teaching and an ease of communication with learner groups. In
this way, initiating and participating in change in work and social
contexts can be seen as a goal of educator development.

Giroux (1991) discusses nine principles of critical pedagogy
that may provide a framework for educators who wish to set social
change goals as a part of their development:

1. Education produces not only knowledge but political awareness, linking education to democracy. Learners are given the
   opportunity to challenge and transform existing social and
   political forms.
2. Ethics is a central concern of educational practice. Ethics and
   politics can be viewed as the relationship between the self and
   the other.
3. Educators should be conscious of differences in two ways: differences among individual learners and differences between
   social groups.

4. Critical pedagogy needs a language that does not reduce issues of power, justice, and inequality to a single script.
5. New forms of knowledge need to be created by breaking down current discipline boundaries.
6. Educators need to be skeptical of reason. The limits of reason should be extended in order to recognize other ways of learning or taking up positions.
7. Critical pedagogy needs to have a sense of alternatives by combining critique and possibility.
8. Educators can be seen as transformative intellectuals who occupy specifiable political and social locations. Critical pedagogy needs to ascertain what the role of teachers can be as cultural workers.
9. Educators need to balance the personal and the political in a way that does not collapse the political into the personal.

Social Change and Educator Development: An Illustration

Tiemo is a nurse educator and the manager of the patient education unit in a large urban hospital. His responsibilities are varied, but they include working with nursing teams to develop materials for patient education, providing resources for health teams, organizing workshops for hospital staff, and sitting on policy-making committees where patient education is an issue.

The hospital has recently undergone a restructuring and flattening of the organizational chart. The position of nurse manager, which was filled by a registered nurse, has now been eliminated and staff nurses report to managers who do not have a nursing background. Nursing education has been broadened to include the interdisciplinary health teams. Nursing assistants have been given a wider range of responsibilities and are required to go to training sessions to prepare for these responsibilities. Most of the staff are anxious, confused, or resentful.

In conjunction with the changes in organizational structure, the hospital has adopted a philosophy of patient self-management. Over the past year, committees have worked to rewrite the mission statement of the hospital and to describe their vision of how patient self-management can be encouraged in diagnosis, the use of medications, and decision making about care plans. One of Tiemo's new responsibilities is to work with staff to make this transition. To this end, he has been working intensively with several health care teams. Through the use of role playing, simulations, and clinical exercises on the hospital floors, he has been helping staff to see just how patient self-management can be encouraged in practice.

Now Tiemo has encountered a serious obstacle to his work. It seems that some proportion of the staff and administration merely espouse patient self-management as a philosophy but do not really see it as feasible. Some of the experienced senior nursing staff, several physicians, a few managers, and many of the technicians from the X-ray lab and the blood lab simply do not think that patients should be making decisions about their care. The staff with whom Tiemo has been working are complaining about this attitude; patients are getting mixed messages.

Tiemo has relatively little power in his organization. He wonders what he should do. In the past, he has never felt obligated to challenge issues; his role has been facilitative and supportive as he has worked with staff.

Tiemo discussed the issue with his health teams, then brought the groups together for a brainstorming and idea session. Several people made the point that the resistant individuals said that there was no reason to believe that patients could participate in their care. "It's just a fad," they had said, "and all you are doing is messing up my routines." "Why not," one nurse asked, "collect some evidence for them? Let's talk to the patients, find out how they feel, write up a report." "Why not," one of the occupational therapists said, "form a team that includes a physician, a technician, a manager?"

An action research project was chosen as a way to foster change in the organization. With enthusiasm, a planning committee (including Tiemo) enticed "disbelievers" to join the research team, and they started selecting methods for finding out how the patient self-management project was actually working.

There will be no easy solution in this case. Watkins and Marsick (1993, pp. 122–123) report on a case where an action research group encountered serious difficulties. That group received mixed responses to their research results and were not at a level in the organization where they could act themselves on the results of their study. The same scenario could evolve for Tiemo's group. However, their inclusion of participants from different levels in the organization may help in this case.

Summary

Education leads to changes—changes in the amount of knowledge people have, changes in skills and competencies, changes in the way we communicate and understand each other, changes in our sense of self, and changes in our social world.

In this chapter, I have examined educators' roles as change agents. In their workplaces, educators can work with their colleagues to develop an understanding of Model I and Model II behaviors, a process that both Argyris and Schön see as the goal of organizational development. Educators can participate in and initiate action research projects in order to examine, question, and change perceptions of practice in the workplace. Feminist pedagogy provides yet another perspective on educators' practice, one that can lead us to look at what we do in a different light.

Amongst ourselves, in our own community of educators, we also have a responsibility to ensure that we are not moving along in a rut, doing what we have always done without questioning or being critical. Professional groups and associations, and discussions of professionalization, are one avenue in which we can raise questions about our practice. Groups for collaborative inquiry present us with another model for working together to critically question our educator roles.

Many practicing educators and education theorists see us as having an important role to play in changing our society at large. We can become involved in political action on a small scale, or we can see it as the focus of all of our work. To some extent, the roles we take on as change agents are a product of our psychological characteristics. Some people are more outgoing and more likely to initiate political movements; other people may prefer to work behind the scenes or to write articles that will focus the thoughts of others.

As educators develop, they are likely to move from the survival skills of being able to organize a session and operate an overhead projector into a stronger interest in social change as a part of their practice. In this way, increased participation in social reform of various kinds is a goal of educator development. I have described one educator who encounters an obstacle in his practice and then starts to work toward organizational change.

Chapter Eight

Creating a New Vision for Professional Growth

Adult educators seem always to have struggled with the notion of who they are. They come into the field along many pathways and tend to identify with their discipline, their context, or their organization rather than with adult education as a profession (see Chapter One). The fact that the professionalization of adult education is a controversial topic supports the view that educators see their differences as being greater than their similarities. Indeed, when one looks at the contexts within which we work and the roles we take on, they are clearly diverse. On the other hand, the process of learning about practice is one that transcends many of our differences. Brockett (1991a, p. 5) suggests that "one way to work toward a common identity is to emphasize an approach to professional development that is not limited solely to mastery of the skills one needs in order to perform effectively. Instead, this approach would emphasize that each of us needs to understand both the 'big picture' of the field and how each of us can make a unique contribution to it."

Historically, professional development for adult educators has focused on the techniques and technical skills required to transmit information or meet learners' expressed needs (see Chapter Two). No theoretical framework or developmental model guided these endeavors. More recently, there has been a call for an understanding of the big picture, as Brockett puts it, and for further conceptualization of adult education in relation to theoretical frameworks. Holford (1995), for example, suggests that adult education is a social movement and as such needs to be situated in a theory of social movements. Griffin (1991) criticizes adult educators for neglecting the sociological perspective, and Brookfield (1993) argues that we have forgotten the political dimensions of our practice. Brockett (1991a, p. 7) believes "that it is crucial for us to create a professional vision that truly characterizes the strengths of our own field, rather than to follow blindly some existing model, such as that found in social work, law, or the health professions."

Actual model development has been minimal. Zuber-Skerritt (1992) presents a model for professional development in higher education, based on action research. The acronym she uses, CRASP, refers to Critical inquiry by Reflective practitioners being Accountable and Self-evaluative, as well as engaged in Participative problem solving. She describes the self-evaluation component as leading to social and personal change and contributing to professionalism (p. 121) but does not actually incorporate social change into the model; rather, it is implied that action research has social change as a goal—a connection made explicit by Kincheloe (1991), for example.

In my earlier writings, I have attempted to formulate two general models of teaching and learning, both with the underlying goal of improved practice. In one (Cranton and Knoop, 1991), a colleague and I focus on higher education. Although we include working conditions and course characteristics as components of the model, we do not go beyond that. In the second, I consider educator development as occurring simultaneously with learner change and both taking place within a learning environment and a social context (Cranton, 1992). However, I was primarily interested in the process of promoting learners' growth. Neither model addresses the concerns raised in the recent literature.

Knox (1992) succinctly points out the importance of including and understanding societal influences by drawing on an international perspective. He argues that professionals' learning is influenced by "transactions between personal characteristics and situational influences from a dynamic external environment" (p. 97). Whether we are interested in understanding educator development in relation to an organization, in the context of our own culture, or within a global perspective, we need to work toward comprehensive models and frameworks in order to integrate these understandings.

In this chapter, I propose a model of influences in educator development—a way of thinking about the different forces that come to bear on our practice and how our changes in our practice, in turn, influence our surroundings. I suggest that individual educators' engagement in critical reflection, self-directed learning, and transformative learning is at the center of the model. These processes are influenced by educators' characteristics and preferences. Teaching context, the organization, and the culture have a further influence on our development. In turn, our development can lead to changes in the teaching context, the organization, and society. I acknowledge that some forms of development are not likely to take place unless they are preceded by social change, but I argue that social change is initiated by people. In the second part of this chapter, I relate my proposed model to some current perspectives in adult education and illustrate each relationship.

A Proposed Model: Overview

I would describe the processes that an individual educator goes through in developing his or her practice as being central to growth and change. In Figure 8.1, I represent this central process as including interactions among critical reflection (CR), self-directed learning (SDL), and transformative learning (TL).

Which comes first, individual or social change, is partially a chicken-and-egg question. At times, educators do not or cannot develop because of the context or culture within which they work; at other times individuals' changes and actions based on their new perspectives stimulate larger-scale developments. Educators do not practice outside of some context and some culture. Their development cannot be unrelated to their environment, but the nature of this relationship is multidimensional.

There are many different ways of conceptualizing these forces and how they work with and against each other in our educational systems. Jarvis (1992b) highlights the many paradoxes between individualism and learning in social contexts. Educational theorists have drawn heavily in recent years on Habermas's understanding of the dimensions of human interests (1971); see, for example, Ewert (1991). From another interesting perspective, Eyerman and Jamison (1991) describe three dimensions or contextualizations of the generation of knowledge through social movements (of which adult education can be considered one). First, the cosmological dimen-

Figure 8.1. Influences on Educator Development.

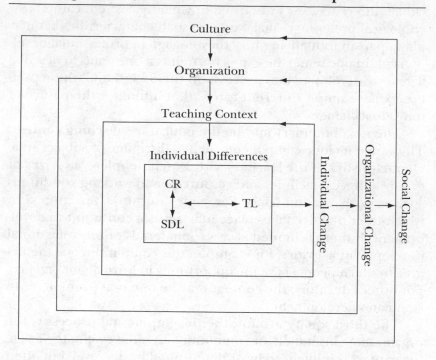

sion represents the beliefs and assumptions shared by participants in the movement, giving them their mission. For adult educators, this dimension could consist of the perspectives of the profession, organization, or community of educators with which they identify. Second, the technological dimension consists of the technical interests (as defined by Habermas, 1971) that are issues for educators. Third, the organizational dimension is the means by which participants organize and put into motion the work that will lead them toward their goals. Formal events and activities, presentations, and workshops—work that takes place within a structure—form the fundamental practice of the educator.

Influences on Educator Development

The first boundary (the innermost square in Figure 8.1) that I have placed around the interaction of critical reflection, self-directed learning, and transformative learning is that of educators' individual differences. As I discussed in Chapter Six, educators' psychological preferences make up one such characteristic that may play a part in influencing how they engage in professional development. In one sense, these are constraints if one wants to describe a generic developmental process; on the other hand, these preferences are simply different forces that influence the nature of individual change.

The next boundary may be the educator's teaching context. This would include components such as discipline or subject area, characteristics of the learners with which people work, sizes of groups, physical facilities and resources, and working conditions such as workload and salary. For some educators, the context in which their practice takes place may act as a constraint to development. If there is limited access to materials or to professional development activities, for example, this could influence the degree to which people have the opportunity to learn about practice. For other educators, the context may be one that promotes and stimulates development.

The third square around the developmental process is the organization, institution, or community. To some extent, the teaching context is influenced by or determined by this level, but often it is not. People may practice within quite different contexts within the same organization. Again, the organization can serve to foster or hinder educators' development, perhaps through its overall culture, perhaps through its reward system.

Finally, all of these layers exist within a culture or society. It is perhaps overly simplistic to depict this as only one boundary, for most of us work in subcultures within larger cultures. My work in a remote mountain area of Tennessee is quite different from a colleague's work in an inner-city community school, though both of us are in a North American culture. My work in a small-town Canadian university bears little resemblance to my colleague's work in a large community college even in the same geographic location. Some of these differences can be accounted for by the organization or community, but others cannot. When we think of the outer boundary, culture, we need to see this also as being in layers. In some cultures or subcultures, growth and development may be fostered, and in others it may not. Classification of the culture itself is not important to this discussion, but the influences of the culture are important.

Educators' Influences on Context, Organization, and Culture

So far, I have described the forces depicted in the model that have an influence on educators' development. When educators develop, they can, in turn, have an influence on the layers in the model. The exception is the first, innermost square of Figure 8.1, referring to individual differences among educators. Here, I do not refer to values, beliefs, or other characteristics which do change through development, but rather to the person's basic nature or personality (see Chapter Six). This is unlikely to change; people may learn to work with their preferences or to develop some preferences over others, but it is usually not a goal of educator development to revise personal psychological preferences.

At the level of their teaching context, educators can and do promote change as a result of their individual development. In the model, this is labeled as individual change at the teaching-context level and as organizational change at the next level. However, these levels cannot be viewed as distinct from one another. Educators who have reflected on and revised their notions of practice are likely to make contextual changes as a part of their development. This can be as simple as room rearrangement or as difficult as challenging their organization's policies. To take some examples, educator development most often leads to changes in methods and strategies, such as a shift to more participatory methods; changes in responsibility for decision making, such as a move toward more learner control; or changes in the content and focus of the learning process, such as an attempt to incorporate more critical thinking and problem solving. Such revisions to practice clearly lead in turn to a change in the teaching context: the sessions are more interactive, learners have more power, or the atmosphere becomes more critical and questioning. The changed teaching context is then a new force for further educator development.

When educators' development is critically reflective or transformative, it will often lead to organizational, institutional, or community change (see Chapter Seven). Even if an educator does not deliberately undertake organizational change, there can be a ripple effect from the revisions one person makes to his or her teaching. Colleagues might observe increased learner enthusiasm and decide to try some of the new methods themselves. Learners sometimes become advocates of strategies they benefited from and challenge other educators to provide the same experience. Senior managers might note the success of middle managers in one unit in utilizing teamwork, question the human resource developer in that area, and encourage other units to take the same approach. Often, too, an educator's change in practice will lead him or her to question organizational policies and procedures, deliberately provoking changes in the system. Group sizes, physical and material resources, evaluation policies, mandatory attendance regulations, and program requirements are just some of the organizational or institutional components that can be shaped through individual educators' efforts. When these changes take place, they again form a modified organizational climate which in turn further stimulates educator development.

A broader-scale social change is more difficult for educators to affect, especially indirectly (see Chapter Seven). The most obvious form that this can take is when the educator's development leads learners to engage in critical questioning of the world around them. Individuals working in, say, literacy education, labor education, environmentalist groups, civil rights movements, or feminist groups are also likely to initiate social change through their own development by virtue of the work they do. On the other hand as I discussed in Chapter Seven, social change need not have such a broad definition, although this is usually not addressed in the literature. A dictionary definition of society is "an organized group of persons associated together for religious, benevolent, cultural, scientific, political, patriotic or other purposes." Culture is described as "the sum total of ways of living built up by a group of human beings and transmitted from one generation to another." Social change may mean changes in the beliefs and assumptions of an organized group of persons or, at the deeper level of cultural beliefs, a change in ways of living. Social change can occur in much the same way as organizational change takes place. If, as a result of his or her development, the educator questions and challenges colleagues, members of professional associations, or members of the community regarding their beliefs about education, then social change can be stimulated. Social changes in turn act as a force that further fosters educators' development.

Although the process of educator development is not linear or cyclical, aspects of the change process feed into and off of each other. For example, an organization is influenced by the culture in which it resides. The organization has some power over the teaching contexts. Individual differences are important within teaching contexts and also influence educators' developmental processes. Educators' changes in their practice can influence their teaching context and therefore some aspects of the organization. All of these developmental processes can affect social change. Each component of the model can influence each other component, and these influences can move in both directions, inward and outward.

Influences on Educator Development and Current Perspectives

Within adult education, a variety of perspectives, philosophies, or frameworks of practice guide our work. A model of the influences on our development should be able to incorporate these different views; that is, regardless of our perspective, we should be able to see what may be some of the critical forces in the process. In this section, I define four of the current perspectives on adult education and examine the relevance of the components of the model for each.

Current Perspectives on Practice

Perspectives on educational practice can be summarized in a variety of ways; no system will contain discrete categories. For example, in his now-classic work on professional education Houle (1980) describes a framework including instruction, inquiry, and performance as the perspectives. Jarvis (1992a) proposes three dimensions of professional knowledge—knowing how, knowing what, and tacit knowledge—and discusses how they are learned. In an earlier book, I categorized adult education perspectives as being subject-oriented, consumer-oriented, and reformist (Cranton, 1994a).

In an informal content analysis of articles in the last three years of the *Adult Education Quarterly* (1992–1995), the last two *Proceedings of the Adult Education Research Conference* (1993 and 1994), and the last three years of the *New Directions in Adult and Continuing Education* series (1992–1995), I found four clusters of perspectives, the first three of which are roughly comparable to my earlier proposal. There was no article or paper presentation that I could not place in at least one, and sometimes two, of the clusters. I do not intend to present this system as definitive; there are a multitude of ways to view our perspectives on practice.

1. *Technical perspectives* include those that employ a traditional instructional design model, have cause-and-effect relationships as underlying assumptions, take a subject-centered approach to teaching and learning, emphasize the transmission of information or the acquisition of skills, or emphasize the technology of instruction and training in some way. Knowledge is viewed, overall, in a positivistic paradigm.

2. *Humanistic perspectives* are people-oriented, learner-centered, or consumer-oriented. They emphasize the importance of the individual and the learning needs of the individual. Individual differences such as learning styles are viewed as important; generally a constructivist paradigm is used to understand knowledge.

3. *Social action perspectives* are reformist and political in nature. They include specific causes such as feminist pedagogies, literacy education, and environmental movements. The goal of educators working in this perspective is empowerment of people oppressed by the constraints placed upon them in their culture. Democratic ideals are usually espoused in this perspective.

4. *Postmodern perspectives* are informed by the interpretive nature of human perceptions, as are the humanist and social action perspectives. They also are based on a perception of the fragmentation of meaning, one in which there is no overall coherence but rather coexisting contradictions. The perspective includes the notion that contemporary communication, especially the pervasiveness of media and electronic communication, has led to an inability to distinguish images from reality.

Educator Development Within Current Perspectives

How would the components of educator development and the various influences on the process be viewed from different philosophies of practice? If we are to find our common identity through learning about practice, as Brockett (1991a) and others suggest, then we should all, regardless of our perspective, be able to identify with some parts of this process. In Table 8.1, for each of the four perspectives defined earlier I suggest how important critical reflection, self-directed learning, transformative learning, individual differences, the teaching context, the organization, and the culture might be from that view of practice.

Technical Perspective

Within a technical perspective, educators' development is primarily the process of acquiring skills and techniques for the efficient transmission of content to students (see Chapter Two). As such, critical self-reflection and transformative learning are less likely to be the central part of a person's development. Self-directed learning, on the other hand, remains a key component, especially in terms of self-management. Most adult educators learn the skills and techniques of their profession through some form of self-directed learning rather than through formal programs or courses. A good example of the kind of resource material adopting this perspective is Piskurich's practical guide to self-directed learning (1993).

Individual differences among educators are not especially important in the technical perspective. Rather, it is assumed that the educator can learn to select the appropriate teaching behavior for the occasion. This does mean, though, that the teaching context is relevant within this framework. The educator adjusts to the characteristics of the group, the setting, and the subject matter. Educator development involves learning how to do this well and becoming quite sophisticated as to which method works best in which situation. Consequently, the nature of the organization or institution also matters—not in the sense that it is to be questioned or challenged, but that the goals, policies, and climate of the organization influence the selection of educational methods. The broader culture or society within which educators work is less relevant here. It may in fact be the culture that supports the paradigm, for example, in terms of the value that the culture places on technology or technical skills, although this is likely to be unarticulated and unquestioned.

An illustration of an educator who holds the technical perspective on practice and development may be helpful. Ottilia

**Table 8.1. Educator Development Within
Current Adult Education Perspectives.**

	Technical	Humanist	Social Action	Postmodern
Critical Reflection	○	○	✓	○
Self-Directed Learning	✓	✓	✓	✓
Transformative Learning	○	✓	○	○
Individual Differences	○	✓	○	✓
Teaching Context	✓	✓	○	○
Organization	✓	○	✓	○
Culture	○	○	✓	✓

Legend: √ important process or influence ○ less important

teaches computing skills, test construction methods, and evaluation procedures to rural, largely untrained public school teachers
in Nigeria. She spent two years in North America to obtain a graduate degree in education and then returned to work in her own
country. Ottilia sees the lack of technological development as one
of the greatest obstacles to improving the education system in
Africa, and this is the primary reason she came to North America:
to obtain some of those skills and pass them on to others.

Since resources, including basic textbooks, are scarce, Ottilia
relies heavily on presenting information verbally to her learners.
She does not have the luxury of computer laboratories, manuals,
or up-to-date equipment. If there is a computer in a school, it has
been donated and it may or may not work reliably. Teachers have
no practical guides or even examples of good evaluation procedures for their students.

When I ask Ottilia about her developmental goals as an educator, she is clear. "I want to be able to organize my presentations,
to explain things clearly, and to prepare useful handouts that the
teachers can rely on after I leave the school." Although she ac-

knowledges the need for social action in the system where she works, Ottilia does not see this as her goal, "at least not for now, at least not until people get some skills."

Humanist Perspective

The humanist perspective has been central to North American adult education for several decades. Within this framework, educators' development is a process of becoming better at interacting with learners, encouraging participation, setting up a warm and inviting atmosphere for learning, and meeting the expressed needs of learners. On the supportive-challenging continuum, support outweighs challenge. As such, critical reflection is less relevant for the humanistic educator's development. It is on this basis that Brookfield (1986) criticized the traditional notion of self-directed learning. Similarly, transformative learning is less important as a goal of development; it is not necessarily the purpose of learning about one's practice to articulate and question assumptions.

Self-directed learning, however, is one of the foundations of humanistic practice, especially in terms of learners making decisions within an educational setting—what Candy (1991) calls the learner-control dimension. One could expect then, that educators practicing within this paradigm would view their own development in a similar way. They would want to be involved in decisions about what they learn.

A consideration of individual differences is also important in the humanistic perspective. Individualism is at the core of humanism. Educators' development would take into account who they are as people, their needs, preferences, and personalities. Similarly, the teaching context would be relevant, including both the context within which the educator works and the context within which the educator learns about his or her practice. The nature of the organization would be primarily a consideration in terms of its influence on the teaching context and general atmosphere. The larger culture supports the humanistic perspective, particularly in North America, but may be less important in its influence on practice.

I illustrate this perspective with the case of John, a new science education teacher in a faculty of education. John taught science in a secondary school for many years before returning to school himself to complete a graduate degree. He loves science, but he says what he loves most is "showing science to others." When he taught secondary school, his work centered around the young people and showing them how they as people were connected to the world of science. Everyone had fun in John's class—impromptu experiments and excursions into the woods in response to a student's question were a part of why science class was so popular.

Now, as a teacher of teachers, John's goal is to "help them have the same enthusiasm and love for the kids as I do." He sees his development as an educator as focusing on his interpersonal skills, his communication with students, and his ability to stimulate interest and excitement in others. He says, "The subject of science is what makes things interesting, but it is secondary really to the people who are learning it." The feelings are reciprocated; John's science teachers-in-training drop into his office continuously to chat and visit, clearly feel comfortable with him, give him high evaluations on all aspects of his teaching, and recommend to their peers that they "try to get into science class, even if [you] don't like science."

I asked John about social change as a goal of his practice, and of his development as an educator, given that science education currently has a strong focus on environmental issues. He agreed that this "was and should be the case" but then said, "my main job is to be a person with them, to be authentic, to care about them, and maybe set off the caring process in them. Maybe they will be the ones to change the world. Not me though; I'm a teacher."

Social Action Perspective

Educators who have a social action perspective on their practice may view their development in a different way from the person who emphasizes the humanistic aspects of working with learners. Since social change requires being aware of assumptions and values, questioning them, and questioning the systems around us, one would expect that critical reflection and transformative learning would also be an important part of the educators' views of development. Self-directed learning, especially in relation to the development of personal autonomy, would also be congruent with this perspective. Empowerment and becoming free from constraints are central concepts in the social action paradigm.

Oddly, individual differences do not seem to be relevant to those educators who see social change as a part of their development. Debates in the transformative learning literature on individual versus social change (Collard and Law, 1989; Mezirow, 1989) highlight this discrepancy in views. It appears that when people work from the social change perspective, individualism is secondary. Although their own growth as an educator will be influenced at least in part by their basic natures, this influence may not be conscious or articulated. Similarly, the details of the teaching context are not often described as relevant to the educator's developmental process in this paradigm.

The organization and the culture provide both a stimulus for development and a target for change. The educator may call himself or herself a critical pedagogue or a critical theorist and see the questioning of the status quo as a goal for both learners and educators. Being able to explicate a theory of practice, question it, and defend it is seen as an important aspect of maturing as an educator. This theory of practice includes an awareness of the organizational or institutional policies and procedures and how they could be changed, as well as a sensitivity to cultural and societal issues.

I illustrate this perspective with the story of Ljerka. She works in a shelter for women who have been victims of abuse, physical or emotional violence, or rape. The shelter is downtown in a large city. She has no formal training as an educator or as a counselor, but she has participated in every professional development activity made available to the shelter staff. Ljerka first became interested in this work when she learned of women of her own cultural background (Eastern European) who seemed to experience conflicts between their own value systems and the values of the North American urban area in which they were now living. The conflicts were related to the value of the family, including the extended family, and especially the role of women in the family.

In terms of her practice, Ljerka saw her main goal as being one of helping the women she worked with become aware that they had options. "It's not that I want to change their values," she said, "but that I want them to have a choice." When I talked to her about her own development, Ljerka wanted to "learn how to change the world." She expressed intense feelings of helplessness and anger. She thought that her lack of formal education would prevent her from being able to "do something." She read extensively, attended talks and workshops, and organized a discussion group for her colleagues at the shelter, all with the goal of developing into a more effective change agent.

Postmodern Perspective

Postmodernists may object to being considered a category in any classification system. As Giroux (1991, p. 17) points out, postmodernism has a "diffuse influence and contradictory character" which does not "lend itself to the usual topology of categories" and "cannot be neatly labeled." However, this is a way of working in adult education practice that is distinctly different from the others I discussed, and educator development will also be different from this viewpoint or set of viewpoints.

It is not my intent here to try to integrate or find consistencies between postmodernism and technical or humanistic perspectives; the gap between these traditions cannot be bridged. The central processes of educator development described here, those of critical reflection and transformative learning, are essentially rational or modernist. Habermas, on whose work Mezirow partly bases transformative learning theory, is one of the leading defenders of rationality (for example, see Habermas, 1983). On the other hand, a key feature of postmodernism is the critique of rationality and universality. Nevertheless, postmodern educators learn about their practice. It is here that one may be able to see some common ground.

One would not expect that educator development in the postmodern perspective would be critically reflective in nature. Critical reflection, as the term has been used here (see Chapter Four), is a rational process. There are, however, some alternative ways of seeing reflection, such as Boyd and Myer's concept of discernment (1988), discussed in Chapter Six, that may be more compatible with postmodernism.

In Table 8.1, I indicate that some form of self-directed learning, specifically Candy's autodidaxy (1991), is relevant in the postmodern perspective. Some postmodern writers in the adult education literature are quite clear about their views of self-directed learning. Collins (1994), for example, equates it with technical rationality and at the same time argues that "to be adult means to be self-directing" (p. 100), using these points to argue that we must shift the focus of our practice away from individualism. Generally, though, it is an incomplete understanding of the multifaceted nature of self-directed learning that can be used to support such arguments. The technical or instrumental view of self-directed learning is now only one representation in the literature.

In autodidactic learning (see Chapter Three for more detail), the individual is not necessarily conscious of being a learner. Autodidaxy is the "noninstitutional pursuit of learning opportunities in the 'natural societal setting'" (Candy, 1991, p. 23). It seems that this aspect of self-directed learning would be in tune with postmodernist educators' development. Although "the modernist view of the individual as an essentially autonomous self-directed entity" (Bagnall, 1995, p. 84) is "problematized" (p. 85) in postmodernism, autodidaxy focuses neither on individualism nor on formal or normative learning.

Individual differences, distinct from individualism, seem to be relevant to the postmodern perspective on education. Bagnall (1995, pp. 81–82) describes a "profound loss of autonomy" and also describes the blurring of the distinctions between "the scholarly and the common, the informed and the ignorant, the highbrow and the low-brow." Unfortunately the language used by postmodern writers is sometimes accessible only to the scholarly, the informed, and the high-brow. Underlying this kind of description is the assumption that individual people, regardless of their position, education, or place in life, are equally important. This is perhaps why the perspectives of postmodernism and feminism are often associated. Giroux (1991, p. 30) writes about "postmodernism's re-theorizing of subjectivity" and sees the self as "constructed as a terrain of conflict and struggle, and subjectivity [as] a site of both liberation and subjugation." Again, one sees an interest in the individual. A reconciliation of psychological type theory (see Chapter Six) and the postmodern perspective may not be possible, however. The language being used to describe postmodern views is primarily indicative of what Jung ([1921] 1971) would call undifferentiation of functions.

Neither the teaching context nor the organization is of particular relevance in the postmodern perspective, in the way they have been described in the educator development model. Both are a part of the normative system which is seriously questioned by the postmodernist, but neither would act as an influence on development, and revisions to this system would not per se be a goal of development.

A rebellion against the broader societal and cultural context is at the heart of postmodernism. Originally a force in art and architecture, postmodernism was a movement against the museum and boardroom views of acceptable art. Now a way of understanding the world around us, the same rebellious and questioning emphasis is there. I would argue that educator development in the postmodern domain is influenced by the culture and has as a goal social change.

I illustrate educator development within the postmodern perspective by describing how Richard learns about his practice. Richard is a part-time adult educator. He teaches self-defense groups through continuing education programs, the Y, or the community center. Richard's primary profession is sculpting, but he loves his teaching and thinks of the two as being in harmony with each other; his students come in some way to see their bodies as sculpture.

When he started teaching several years ago, Richard saw it as only a way to make a little money to support his work as an artist. He ran his groups in a very mechanistic way, showing people how to respond to physical threat in different ways and then having them practice the moves until they became smooth and almost automatic.

Richard started to see his teaching practice differently when he first noticed that students' initial response to a simulated defense was to be passive, virtually give up before they had tried. He discussed this with a small group of women from his class, and they described a physical, emotional, and intellectual reaction of powerlessness and helplessness. They could not or did not separate their bodies' responses from their feelings of being a victim or from their rational knowledge that they could do something. As hard as he worked with this group, that separation was not achieved. They did learn the physical responses, but they still seemed trapped by their minds. Richard felt that he was separated from understanding his students by being male, by not knowing their fear of violence and aggression in the "very fibre of their being," as the students expressed it. No amount of analysis was helpful to him; no amount of reflection or discussion changed the students' perspective.

Richard's change in perspective came to him as "a profound sense of insight." One day, he saw the students in his class as a sculpture. The lines and shapes of their bodies reflected their fears and feelings and power as clearly as the lines of a sculpture. He did not, at this time, know what to do with this perception, but he felt it was a way for him to change his practice.

Richard began trying various approaches to his practice. He asked learners to draw how they felt; he led extended role-playing sessions in which people fought a "real mugger"; he played violent music during the sessions; he displayed slides of sexist advertisements on the walls of his classroom. Richard expressed his own feelings to his class and showed them photographs of his sculptures depicting powerlessness. His teaching changed and is still changing dramatically. He asked for and has read articles on feminist pedagogy and postmodernism. The latter, especially McLaren's (1991) notion of enfleshment, connected to Richard's perception of his development once he was able to adapt to the academic language of the reading.

I asked Richard to describe how he learned about teaching. He had some difficulty in responding. He saw that his goal had developed from one of just teaching "the mechanics" to one of wanting "to erase powerlessness, to help eliminate the differences between groups of people, women and attackers." He said that there was no "systematic way" that he learned, but rather that he had "things come from just being there, in the experience, and seeing, and feeling what they feel, and then knowing what to do." At one point, Richard said, "I'm not sure I learn anything really, I just get it or I don't and sometimes you give me an article and I don't read it but sometimes I do. I don't really learn, as you mean it." I asked him about social change as a goal of his practice. He was mildly surprised. "Of course, it is all about social change, isn't it? But I don't suppose I change anything in the social context. At best, a few people see themselves as not so powerless. At worst, they learn how to hit back. And that's not so bad. That could be social change, too, couldn't it?"

Summary

Every person learns about what he or she does when this "doing" is experienced over time or in different settings or with different people. Some kinds of experiences lead to nonreflective knowledge, such as in primitive psychomotor learning. Some kinds of experiences lead to nonreflective action (Mezirow, 1991): habitual action such as driving a car, thoughtful action such as analysis or judgment, or introspection such as being aware of enjoying an event. The educator who is learning about practice may well be perfecting skills and techniques, developing habitual actions, engaging in problem solving and analysis, and being aware of the experience. Indeed, for many educators, this may form a large part of their learning about teaching; when it is "done," their development stops.

This is not to say that the acquisition of skills for effective practice is not a necessary part of professional development. But perhaps what distinguishes a profession from skills-based work is what Schön (1987) calls professional artistry. The educator seems to respond in spontaneous ways to complex and often contradictory sets of circumstances. Schön attributes this ability to reflection-in-action.

In this chapter, I have presented educators' professional development as a process of critical self-reflection and self-directed learning, potentially leading to a revision of one's assumptions about teaching or one's larger perspectives on education. Centra (1993, p. 175) quotes Marvin Bressler, a Princeton professor, as saying that teachers must not describe their success as a clever performance, so to speak, but rather "by their contribution to the transformation of students" and by the "expanding and deepening students' comprehension of the universe, intellectual and moral." If we accept this laudable goal, then it seems that we also accept learning about teaching as a transformative process.

Educators' different characteristics, including their psychological type, learning style, past experiences, and values, to name but a few, play a role in determining how learning and development occurs for them, as I discussed in Chapter Six. Similarly, differences in the context within which people teach have an influence on how they develop. An educator's discipline, physical environment, group size, and working conditions may enhance or hinder learning.

On a larger scale, the organization, institution, or community where the education takes place will have some impact on the direction and degree of educators' development, either through the teaching context or through other characteristics of the organization. At an even broader level, the culture or subculture, including the values placed on education and learning, act as a force on development.

There is no linear set of variables influencing professional development for educators. Each of the levels mentioned in this chapter influences the others and is, in turn, affected by educators' learning. Educator development leads to changes in the organization and broader social changes, just as those changes can then lead back to further learning for the educator.

The adult education literature remains divided into various perspectives. There are those who are primarily interested in training and the acquisition of technical skills and who view self-directed learning as an efficient way to instrumental learning. There are those who follow in Malcolm Knowles's footsteps and retain the humanistic view of education as meeting personal needs. There are those who have resurrected the original goals of adult education, empowerment of individuals and change in social structures. And recently, there is the postmodern view in which rationality is rejected.

Brockett (1991a) suggests that it may be through professional development that the fragmentation of adult education practice can be addressed. In this chapter, I have examined the influences on educator development through each of the four perspectives found in the literature. No one perspective contained all elements of the model, but each element was relevant to one or more perspectives. It may well be that we can come to understand our individual theoretical differences through reflection on how we learn about our practice. That we all learn professionally may be the universal factor in adult education.

Chapter Nine

Strategies for the Developer

The assumption that adult educators are self-directed and reflective learners of their practice is maintained throughout this book. What about those professionals who work with educators to facilitate their development? What is their role? In Chapter Two, I argued that one of the reasons some traditional developmental strategies are not as effective as they could be is that developers try to transmit knowledge about teaching rather than encourage reflection on practice. In Chapters Three, Four, and Five, I presented strategies that educators could use in their own development. Many organizations, however, have people employed to help educators learn about practice. In this chapter, I revisit the themes of the previous chapters and examine their implications for those of us who are "developers."

Educators often look for simple guidelines, want to be told, and expect expertise to be transmitted. Indeed, we often need to learn technical skills and techniques. There is not much point in being critically reflective if a person turns his back to the group and mumbles incoherently. Autonomous self-directed learning may not be the most effective way to learn how to prepare a set of handouts for a workshop. Educators need to learn technical skills just as an artist needs to learn about brush strokes and drawing techniques. When does the developer transmit expertise, and when does she question and challenge? When does the developer hand out resources, and when does he encourage reflection? When do developers work toward changing the policies or structures of their organization? These are among the issues I discuss in this chapter.

Who are the professional developers for educators of adults? One defined group of developers is that known as "trainers of trainers" (see Chapter Two). This group also has a home in terms of professional identification: that they emphasize technical skills and instrumental learning is a part of the business-and-industry context within which they work.

Another clearly identifiable contingent of developers includes those who work with faculty in colleges and universities. They call themselves instructional or faculty developers; they have a literature, journals, and professional associations. Instructional developers tend not to see themselves as associated with adult education, but as I have argued elsewhere (Cranton, 1994b) the theoretical frameworks of self-directed and transformative learning can provide a foundation for practice in this field.

There are nurse educators who work to help nurses learn how to engage in patient education. More generally, continuing professional education consultants and program planners devise developmental programs, workshops, and activities for medical, paramedical, dental, physiotherapy, and other health professionals.

Adult education practitioners themselves can become developers. For example, people working in adult basic education programs who come to be recognized for their expertise in an area (literacy training, curriculum planning, evaluation) often train other educators.

Continuing education and graduate programs in adult education provide developmental work for practitioners. However, these fields are scattered and fragmented; there is no one forum for developers of adult educators, as would be expected given that there is no *one* profession. In higher education, instructional development is beginning to turn into a field of scholarly inquiry and practical guidance. In the health professions, some integration of adult education and professional practice is yielding helpful guidance for developers, but this is in a rather neophyte stage. Otherwise, professional developers appear to be on their own.

In this chapter, I bring together the concepts of self-directed learning, critical reflection, and transformative learning to provide some strategies that developers can use in working with educators. I maintain that the organizational and social contexts influence the work we do and that we in turn affect organizational and social change through our endeavors. I have chosen some specific strategies to discuss: individual consultation with educators, action research, working with groups, and organizational development.

Individual Consultation

Most organizations having a position for educational development expect the one person in that position to provide service to a fairly large number of educators. Even when emphasis is placed on quality of teaching, as is currently the case in higher education (see Quinlan, 1991), this espoused value is not well-supported with funding, staff, resources, or facilities. Consequently, individual consultation between educators and developers is seen as somewhat of a luxury. The tendency is to attempt to prove cost-effectiveness by processing large numbers of clients as recipients of workshops, presentations, and how-to materials. Centra (1993, p. 176) quotes an old adage that is also appropriate here: "Not everything that counts can be counted, and not everything that can be counted counts."

If we agree that encouraging critical reflection, self-direction, and transformative learning are central processes in educator development, then one-on-one discussions between educator and developer have a strong potential for facilitating growth. Mezirow (1991, p. 197) writes that the goal of emancipatory education is "to help learners move from a simple awareness of their experiencing to an awareness of the *conditions* of their experiencing (*how* they are perceiving, thinking, judging, feeling, acting—a reflection on process) and beyond this to an awareness of the *reasons why* they experience as they do and to action based upon these insights." Such a goal is also one that counselors would express. Tennant (1993) makes a clear and convincing argument for individual and social development being linked in transformative learning theory. For the time being, I turn to the individual-consultation component of educator development; I return to group and organizational strategies in the remaining sections of this chapter.

In order for individual consultation between educator and developer to be effective in fostering reflection and transformation, it needs to be long-term, critical, and experiential.

Length of Consultation

Developers are familiar with the notion of educators consulting them with short-term needs: "How should I prepare this session?" "Can you give me some materials on time management?" Such requests we respond to, of course. However, I argue that our goal should be to entice educators who have short-term requests into longer-term consultations, and in general to encourage people to work with us over time. Becoming aware of a theory of practice, explicating assumptions about teaching, and questioning and possibly revising those assumptions cannot take place in one or two sessions.

The developer first needs to gain an in-depth understanding of the educator's teaching and organizational context. Even if the two individuals are working in the same organization, institution, or community, there may well be different policies, values, and climates between one part of the setting and another. It is useful for the developer to meet with the educator in the educator's work space—office, classroom, or even home—so as to absorb some of that atmosphere. Observing the educator work with learners is also valuable, although this can be intimidating for some people when it is suggested too early in the consultation process.

Becoming familiar with the materials, resources, activities, and readings used by the educator also increases the developer's understanding of the context. This need not be treated as a review or assessment of materials, unless that is a part of the consultation, but rather as a way of enhancing awareness of the educator's practice. Of course, developers are not, and need not be, experts in the educator's discipline. They will, however, through practice and experience attain an understanding of the structure or nature of knowledge in different subject areas.

Ongoing discussions between the developer and the educator form the central component of the consultation. Initially, the focus of these discussions will be on the developer learning about the educator's practice. The developer works in a supportive, listening, empathetic role as he or she learns about the teaching context. The emphasis of the discussions needs to move gradually to a more challenging and critical level as time goes on.

How long is long-term consultation? This is dependent on the content and nature of the interaction, but three or four months of regular meetings might be the minimum amount of time to foster critical reflection on practice.

Critical Consultation

When the developer has gained a good understanding of the educator's practice, and when trust and rapport have been established between the two individuals, then the supportive-challenging balance can shift to the challenging side. The developer who is only supportive or who works solely to meet the educator's expressed needs may not stimulate critical reflection.

As Brookfield (1987) points out, the word *critical* has an unnecessarily negative connotation in our society. People do not like to be critical and do not like others to be critical of them; it can be "highly intimidating" and "threatening to our sense of self" (Brookfield, 1987, p. 17). On the other hand, critical reflection or critical thinking can be positive and productive. "Critical thinkers are actively engaged with life. They see themselves as creating and recreating aspects of their personal, workplace, and political lives. They appreciate creativity, they are innovators, and they exude a sense that life is full of possibilities" (Brookfield, 1987, p. 5). It is through critical questioning and challenge that educators will be moved to consider alternatives to their current methods. If I ask one educator, for example, his rationale for using multiple-choice testing, or if I ask another person why she sets up a "teacher's desk" in the room even though it is an informal setting, my questions can lead to an opening up of choices. "Maybe I could use a different test format," or "I never even thought of it as the teacher's desk," the educators could say. When this happens—whether or not people actually change their practice—they have become free of the constraint of not knowing that there are alternatives. Ultimately, this should be a goal of professional development. It is not that we engage in any one practice because we do not know alternatives, but rather because we have deliberately chosen that way from among several alternatives.

At this stage in consultation, the developer benefits from observing the educator in practice. There can be a discrepancy between what the educator says he or she does and actual practice (as described by Schön, 1987). Critical consultation simply means asking the educator to talk about practice—what is being done, how that method was chosen, and why this is important to discuss. For example, a teacher in an adult basic education program may describe herself as a people-person, a humanist who cares about the students. She may see that she adopted that approach to practice because she went through such a program herself and felt that her life was changed by a caring teacher. She may realize that it is important to have this understanding, as she has the tendency to want to change all her students' lives and this is unrealistic. These are the components of content reflection, process reflection, and premise reflection that Mezirow (1991) sees as the basis of transformative learning.

Ideally, through critical consultation, the educator is able to articulate his or her theory of practice, question its source, and describe its consequences. Such articulation will often lead a person to make changes, but it may not. The decision to revise assumptions and perspectives about teaching is always the educator's. The developer's goal is to help make options available.

Experiential Consultation

Recently, a new professional developer enthusiastically described a "high" in her practice. He wrote, "I have known these things theoretically, in the abstract, but then I suddenly saw them *in practice* with a client and everything fell into place. I never knew what these things really meant before." Effective consultation is experiential. The developer cannot be a holder of abstract knowledge about teaching and still relate to educators who are practicing. Ideally, the developer also works with learners in some way, but this may be less important than becoming involved with clients' practice.

I suggested earlier that developers should observe educators working with learners; that is one way of engaging in experiential learning about practice. Watching videotapes of the client's practice and discussing them with the client provides similar involvement but adds the dimension of reflection through discussion. Developers can also hold discussion groups with learners, become involved in program planning, meet with employers or other members of the community to discuss the goals of a particular program, volunteer their time in learning centers, initiate their own action groups, or act in any similar way to learn about educators' experiences.

Experience, or acting on one's learning, is a component of most conceptualizations of learning. Transformative learning theory includes action as a component (Mezirow, 1991). In his presentation of the DATA (*Describe, Analyze, Theorize, Act*) model of reflective practice, Peters (1991, p. 95) says that "without action, all of the previous work remains theoretical, and not much changes." He emphasizes that the action becomes a subject for further reflection and analysis; the process is like a spiral. On one level, for the professional developer, practice is working with educators, but on a deeper level, it is experiencing the teaching and learning practice of the client and working with that experience. In one Canadian university, a professional development program for college instructors is being changed to a distance education program; the developer will not have the opportunity to experience the educators' practice or even engage in face-to-face discussion of their practice. Such an approach removes a vital aspect of development work.

Action Research

Action research was described in Chapter Seven as a means of promoting social change in adult education. Action research has its origins in the work of Kurt Lewin (1948), who was dedicated to integrating theory and practice, inquiry and social change. Lewin and his colleagues rejected the experimental research methods that were popular at the time and engaged in what they called experiential phenomenology, paying careful and close attention to the meaning that a situation had for a person and describing the psychological processes involved.

Over the next decades, the concept of action research was interpreted in odd ways by people writing about research methodologies. One of the less questionable but still incongruent definitions is given by Best and Kahn (1986, p. 22), who write: "Action research is focused on immediate application, not on the development of theory or on general application. It has placed its emphasis on a problem here and now in a local setting."

Recently, action research has been revived as a means of professionals' engaging in critical reflection on their practice (Zuber-Skerritt, 1992) and as a path to empowerment for educators (Kincheloe, 1991). Kincheloe, especially, describes action research as a process that "revolutionizes traditional conceptions of staff development, making it a democratic, teacher-directed activity rather than a manifestation of the hierarchical imposition of the bad workplace" (pp. 16–17).

For the professional developer, action research is a means of working with educators to understand and learn about their practice while simultaneously fostering educators' learning and development. Lewin (1948, pp. 202–203) originally defined action research in this way: "The research needed for social practice can best be characterized as research for social management or social engineering. It is a type of action research, a comparative research on the conditions and effects of various forms of social action, and research leading to social action. Research that produces nothing but books will not suffice."

Kincheloe (1991, pp. 108–110) defines action research as containing the following processes:

- Constructing a system of meaning related to practice
- Understanding dominant research methods and their effects
- Selecting what to study
- Acquiring a variety of research strategies
- Making sense of information collected
- Gaining awareness of the tacit theories and assumptions that guide practice
- Viewing teaching as an emancipatory, praxiological act

Following a slightly different philosophical orientation, Angelo and Cross (1988) advocate a model of action research based on the notion that the research is motivated by a "teacher's desire to learn more about student learning in order to improve teaching" (p. 11). They make five assumptions:

1. The best way to improve student learning is to improve teaching.
2. Teachers need to make their objectives explicit and need to receive specific feedback on the extent to which they reach these objectives.
3. Teachers should conduct research on questions derived from their own practice.
4. Classroom research provides intellectual challenges that motivate teachers.
5. Everyone who is dedicated to teaching can engage in classroom research.

The literature contains several examples of articles based on action research, although they are not easy to track. They tend to originate in higher education and are usually published in journals devoted to teaching in a specific discipline. Nevertheless, professional developers might find it worthwhile to review some examples as models. Brandt and Sell (1986) describe a study of problem-solving skills among engineering students. Peters (1994) describes seven community college instructors who engaged in collaborative inquiry in order to improve their practice; the process was described as having a profound impact on the educators' professional growth.

At Brock University in Canada, Kreber (1995) has implemented a program in which the developer works with the educator in a team approach to conduct action research on the educator's practice. It is this kind of activity that can be used by developers to foster critically reflective development. Together, the developer and the educator consider the questions about practice that could be investigated. The developer has expertise in the teaching and learning process and a knowledge of the theoretical foundations of that practice. The educator has expertise in teaching in the discipline as well as firsthand experience of the teaching context and the organization. They pose a research question that is both sensible in terms of theory and practical in terms of the educator's needs—Lewin's notion of the integration of theory and practice. They then work collaboratively to carry out the research using, as Kincheloe (1991) suggests, a variety of research methodologies. Action research need not be restricted to any one research paradigm. The educator learns about his or her practice, the developer learns about educator practice, and ideally, the results of the research are disseminated to the larger community of educators, where others will gain insight into their practice.

Working with Groups

Educators' practice is essentially a matter of communication and of working with groups. When we teach, we are presenting and explaining concepts, clarifying the structure of knowledge, questioning others, facilitating discussion among people, and encouraging critical reflection. Professional developers have a tendency to minimize the power of groups. Yet a group of educators who meet regularly over an extended period of time, and who develop trust and confidence in each other, may be more likely to stimulate critical reflection on their practice than is the developer working alone with an educator or leading a one-time discussion.

There are many strategies for working with groups. I discuss formalized courses, informal discussion groups, collaborative inquiry, and management or administrative teams.

Courses

One of the first responses of educators who are contemplating sustained learning over time is to prefer the framework of a formal course. Zeph (1991, p. 79), for example, describes graduate school as existing "for the purpose of professional development." Although this definition of graduate studies could certainly be questioned, there is no doubt that educators often turn to formal courses and programs for development.

How can the professional developer take advantage of this tendency? The developer who works within a college or university can offer a course on teaching and learning in higher education, as is done at several institutions. Such a course can be available for credit for graduate teaching assistants, or faculty if they should want credit, or it can be a noncredit course which still appears on transcripts or is formally documented in some way.

Developers working in other organizations can offer a formal course as well. They might award a certificate upon completion of the course, a document that an educator can put into the dossier or add to the curriculum vitae. They might also make arrangements for their course to be awarded continuing-education hours with professional licensing boards, as does CareerTrack (1995). Sometimes arrangements can be made with local colleges, school boards, or universities to give credit for courses offered at other institutions. Formal credit can be intrinsically motivating, or it can help the educator to achieve promotion, salary increases, and the like.

Discussion Groups

I advocate discussion groups as a way for educators to reflect on their practice. Professional developers can initiate discussion groups among the educators with whom they work. To give one example, Amundsen, Gryspeerdt, and Moxness (1993) describe a process they call practice-centered inquiry. One aspect of their process is a loosely structured discussion group in which educator's interests and issues are addressed. The groups meet twelve to fourteen times.

Discussion groups are considered to be invaluable to learning in any milieu, and guidelines for the maintenance and support of effective groups are commonly available in the literature on adult education. Wlodkowski (1990, pp. 202–203) summarizes the characteristics of an effective learning group:

- A people-centered learning environment, one that is caring, warm, informal, and respectful of each individual
- A high level of trust, where people are open to sharing information, ideas, thoughts, feelings, and reactions to the issues being addressed
- An ease of communication, with people listening to one another and being accessible for dialogue
- A collaborative atmosphere in which cooperation overrides competitiveness as a group value
- An acceptance of personal responsibility, with people holding themselves accountable for their choices and behavior
- Clear and accepted learning goals, where members of the group understand and value the goals of the meetings

Ideally, the developer would help to start or to organize educator discussion groups but would not necessarily lead or facilitate them. If our goal is self-directed and reflective learning about practice, the responsibility for the learning needs to shift to the educators themselves (Cranton, 1994b).

Collaborative Inquiry

Collaborative inquiry was discussed in Chapter Seven as one strategy for individuals who see social change as a goal of adult education. For the developer, collaborative inquiry can be viewed as a combination of working with groups and action research. If, in the organization, there is already an interest in issues such as program planning or evaluation of educational services, the developer can facilitate the development of teams or groups of educators to investigate the issues of interest. The developer's role might be to bring together people who want to work on the topic and to help set an agenda. Again, ideally the developer would withdraw, leaving the educator team to work together.

In some settings, there may be educators with different kinds of subject area expertise who are concerned about the same teaching and learning problem—for example, how to motivate learners, how to evaluate learning, how to use technology in teaching. Cross-disciplinary teams or committees can bring together diverse perspectives to address the area of interest. The developer can help set up the group, initiate the discussion, provide some ideas as to the form that the inquiry should take, and then leave the group to work on their own.

Collaborative inquiry can also take place among developers within the same organization or across different settings. Say a group of developers are concerned about the strategies they use with educators; they can set up a collaborative inquiry team to investigate their own practice, perhaps conducting action research into their practice. Such an experience can simultaneously provide a model that the developers can use in working with educators.

Working with Organizations

Educational developers sometimes view themselves as being primarily responsible to the individual client. Yet as I discussed in Chapter Eight, educators work within and are influenced by teaching contexts that are, in turn, within organizational structures and climates. The developer needs not only to be aware of these influences but also to work to create a climate that is conducive to good practice. Sometimes this requires an active reformer role; at other times it is simply a matter of being involved in the workings of the organization.

Policies and Procedures

People in an organization develop policies, procedures, rules, and routines that are intended to make the organization run smoothly. It is not always the case that such policies enhance educational practice. When the primary function of the organization is not education, such as in government departments, hospitals, or businesses, the policy makers are likely not to be thinking about education when they consider the ramifications of a particular guideline. Even when the primary function is education, such as in colleges and universities, policy makers in, say, a registrar's office may be trying to ensure the smooth flow of papers and forms through their office rather than the best process for the educator and the learner. In any system, people will want to make their part of that system work well; not many see the whole picture at once.

Developers can question policies and procedures whenever they appear to be working at cross-purposes to educator practice. It may just be a matter of informing policy makers as to the consequences of certain regulations. For example, a policy requiring that educators submit a full description of a course or program months in advance of their meeting the students may violate educators' desires to implement self-directed learning strategies, but policy makers may not be aware of the concept of developing instruction with learners. On the other hand, policies tend to be reified: because they have existed in the past, this is why they should continue to be followed. The common explanation of "they say . . ." without an understanding of who "they" might be is indicative of this phenomenon. The developer's responsibility then is to critically question the source and the consequences of such policies.

We often are in the position of trying to remedy situations of which we were not originally a part. But ideally, the developer should be involved in the design of policies and procedures that are relevant to educational practice. Offering to provide information, expertise, and resources to policy makers is helpful. Copies of research or theoretical articles will not be too useful to people without expertise in education; rather, the developer can write or use summaries that employ ordinary language. There are good sources of such materials, such as the newsletter *The Teaching Professor* or the magazine *Adult Learning*. When possible, it is usually best to write short, jargon-free materials that take into account the context of the organization.

Committees

One of the most effective ways to promote organizational development that is congruent with educator development is to participate in the committees or teams responsible for the relevant issues. It is rare that a committee will refuse a new member if that person offers to bring a new perspective to the mandate of the committee. Depending on the situation and the place of the committee in the hierarchy of the organization, one may need to offer to be a nonvoting member or even an observer; nevertheless it is quite possible to be heard at the policy-making level of committee work. If it is necessary to be sponsored or recommended to a committee, that too is worthwhile.

Once the developer is involved in committees relevant to educational policy, it again becomes important to maintain the dual role of informing others and questioning current practices. Being a rabble-rouser is not helpful; the developer has one expertise while other members of the organization have their own. Clear and confident communication is called for, backed up by resources, guides, and available research evidence. One useful role that a professional developer can take in many policy-making committees is that of collecting information about education and learning in the organization. This may take the form of, for example, a learning needs assessment or survey, compiling data on existing practices, describing the prevalent values toward education, or even examining social influences on the organization's educational goals. As committees often seem to find themselves in the position of making decisions and recommending policy without adequate information, such a role can be greatly appreciated.

Developers can also initiate committees relevant to particular concerns they have. A group voice is usually more powerful than a lone voice, particularly if that group represents various levels or sectors of the organization. In a hierarchical or structured organization, this strategy may not be as successful; it may be necessary to obtain approval for the committee. If it is an ad hoc informal committee, it may not be heard. Still, the avenue is worth pursuing. Committees, task forces, or teams may be very effective in working toward change in more informal institutions or in a community.

Professional Associations

Working with professional associations was suggested in Chapter Seven as a means for adult educators to work toward social change. For developers who are interested in enhancing the context within which educators work, professional associations can also be relevant.

Developers should inform educators about professional associations they may be interested in. Educators of adults are often not aware that such associations exist, since they identify with their discipline rather than with education. An environment in which such information is routinely shared contributes to the value that people place on their teaching practice. Sometimes through professional associations developers can encourage educators to engage in action research on their practice, including the writing of articles about practice.

Educators can also be encouraged to promote educational issues within professional associations related to their subject area. They might be interested in initiating a special interest group in, for example, the teaching of mathematics or in dentistry education within an association usually devoted to pure research and theory in the discipline. Another activity that can be encouraged is submitting proposals for funding or for conference sessions on teaching, to associations normally outside of education.

If groups of people begin to advocate educational interests in their profession, this energy is likely to carry over into the teaching climate of the organization. Administrative support may then be increased, possibly through funding to attend conferences or the provision of resources to set up special interest groups. Action research may be encouraged and spontaneous discussion groups may occur.

Networks

In Chapter Seven, I suggested participation in networks as a strategy for educator development. The professional developer can facilitate such participation by making information about existing networks available and by encouraging educators to set up their own networks. In Canada, the Society for Teaching and Learning in Higher Education initiated an electronic mail discussion group on educational issues; an instructional development person acts as the coordinator for this network. Educators from many disciplines across North America are now involved, and the issues dealt with are wide-ranging. Many such networks are available on the Internet.

Within an organization, the developer can encourage local networks: discussions on electronic mail regarding issues of specific interest to educators in that context, or linkages through face-to-face interactions such as exist in peer consultation programs. Critical reflection on one's practice is encouraged by discussion and questioning. Networks serve this purpose very well as people tend to connect with others who share interests and perspectives.

At times, computer-conference courses or programs may be available on topics in adult education. If the developer can encourage educators to participate, the contacts made can form into educational networks upon completion of the more formal activity of the course. If several people from one organization become involved, they may find themselves with an informal network during and following the course.

Individual Differences Among Educational Developers

Professional developers have different teaching and learning preferences. Just as we often mistakenly assume that educators can easily adjust themselves to the personalities and preferences of their students, so do we assume that developers have an array of styles and strategies that they can pull out of their briefcases as the need arises. This belief may even be exacerbated by the knowledge that

developers have expertise in teaching and learning—since they
know about variations in styles, they should be able to use each
style with equal ease. Developers vary, of course, not only in their
comfort with styles but also in their own philosophies of practice
and their assumptions about the goals of adult education.

In Chapter Six, I discuss individual differences among educators based on Jung's theory of psychological type ([1921] 1971). In
this section, I suggest some possible relationships among psychological type and preferences for developmental strategies. I briefly
examine each of the strategies presented in this chapter: individual
consultation, action research, working with groups, and organizational development. The suggestions are based on theory and on
my experience in working with psychological type preferences.

Individual Consultation

In individual consultation with educators, there is the widest scope
for differences among developers. Each person will adopt his or
her personal style in working with others. It is only if there is a
strong clash of preferences that a developer may have some difficulty. If he or she is aware of individual differences, it is usually possible to work collegially with a client who has a quite different
personality. However, the nature of the interaction could be influenced by the developer's type preferences. Since it is usually the
developers who lead or guide the conversation and the issues
addressed, it is their personality that has the most potential to
direct the course of the interactions.

Developers who prefer using the thinking function could tend
to be logical and analytical in their approaches to working with
clients. They might emphasize the organization and structure of
the session or course over the educator's rapport with students. It
is possible that they would have limited patience or understanding
of clients who are enthusiastically going off on seemingly unrelated
tangents in a discussion or those who seem to overemphasize facts
and information.

A preference for the feeling function leads developers to use
values rather than logic in decision making. They might see a
client's work as "just feeling right" and be unable to explain why
they make the judgments they do. Their reactions to an educator's

practice could be based on the climate of harmony in the session. They could discourage critical questioning or challenging as being contradictory to the development of a good classroom climate.

Developers who prefer the intuitive function could de-emphasize the importance of organization or structure in their clients' practice and rather look for creativity, imagination, and future-oriented discussions. They could discourage the presentation of facts and overlook the importance of experiential learning.

When the sensing function is preferred by developers, they may not appreciate open-ended or seemingly wandering discussions. Unless they also share a preference for thinking as an auxiliary function, they may not address issues of organization or relations among topics with their clients. Similarly, unless they have a secondary feeling function, they might de-emphasize interpersonal relationships in clients' practice.

Whether developers are primarily extraverted or introverted is relevant to a lesser extent in individual consultations. The developer who is more introverted could be, for example, less likely to offer to visit the client's practice and hold discussions with students, and the developer who is more extraverted could encourage the client to engage in outgoing strategies that are not suitable if the educator is not so extraverted.

Action Research

The goals of action research incorporate all psychological type preferences. One wants to come to an analytical understanding of practice (thinking) in order to improve that practice (intuition) using collaborative methods (feeling) based on experience of the practice (sensing). Some components of action research should appeal to all professional developers and educators, regardless of their psychological preferences. Those who write about action research may emphasize one aspect of the approach over another; for example, Kincheloe (1991) stresses social action as a goal, an area of interest to people with an extraverted intuitive preference.

Developers might use slightly different approaches to action research dependent on their own styles. They could emphasize the collaborative aspect by bringing together groups of educators to work on a project. For others, the experiential or practical component might be the most important. Regardless, unlike some other developmental strategies action research has the potential to appeal to a wide range of individuals.

Working with Groups

Working with others is more comfortable for people who are more extraverted. In the current climate of teamwork and participatory decision making, avoiding groups is all but impossible. Even if it does not come naturally, most people have learned to work with groups. Based on psychological type theory, one would predict that a tendency toward extraverted feeling would lead to the strongest interest in working with groups. Conversely, an inclination toward introverted thinking could lead to discomfort in groups. However, the nature of group work is also relevant.

Courses, workshops, and seminars can have a more structured format and be more in tune with a thinking function preference. In fact, the developer's style or preference can shape the nature of a course. This is an advantage for the developer, but it may create some conflict for participants; for example, the creative intuitive rambling of a developer can be frustrating for the down-to-earth practical participant.

Discussion groups tend to emphasize rational argumentation and critical questioning. As such, they will be enjoyed by the professional developer who prefers the thinking function. Collaborative inquiry groups, on the other hand, are likely the forte of individuals with a preference for the feeling function, since they stress belonging and group membership as purposes.

Working with management and administrative groups has organizational improvement as a goal and is therefore most likely to be appealing to developers who have a preference for intuition. Extraverted developers in general will not mind this aspect of their work; those people who are more introverted will be less comfortable.

Working with Organizations

The promotion of organizational change fits well with the inclinations of extraverted intuition. The intuitive tendency is toward seeing how things could be rather than how they are, and extraversion provides the interest in the outside world. This aspect of professional development would not be easy for feeling types who dislike creating conflict. It would also be different for most people who are more introverted than extraverted because it involves imposing oneself and one's views on the external environment.

Summary

Although many adult educators develop their practice on their own or in discussions with colleagues, professional developers have a meaningful role to play. They may be more visible in higher education than in other areas, but they can be found training trainers, developing programs in business, teaching in continuing education, or working in human resource development units. How can they promote self-directed and transformative educator development?

In this chapter, I have provided an overview of some strategies that developers can use in working with educators. Individual consultations, though time-consuming and expensive, have the potential to be very effective in fostering critical reflection on practice. This is especially true if the consultation takes place over a longer period of time and involves critical questioning of the educator's practice. When consultation is connected with practice through the developer's experience with the educator's work, the exchange will be more meaningful for both individuals.

Action research has considerable potential for educational development. The developer and an educator or a group of educators can work together to address research questions about the effectiveness of practice and ways to improve practice.

Most of what educators do involves working with groups. Similarly, developers view group interactions as central to their work. This may take the form of more formal courses or series of sessions on teaching and learning, or it may take place in more informal discussion groups. Collaborative inquiry can promote critical reflection on practice, especially when people from different disciplines or areas are brought together. Developers can also work with management or administrative groups to encourage changes that are conducive to educators' work.

Professional development also involves working toward organizational development. It is often the constraints, policies, and procedures of the workplace that hinder educator growth. By influencing these policies and working on policy-making committees, the developer can do much to help the educator. Professional associations and networks play a part in organizational life. A developer can take various initiatives to promote others' involvement in such activities.

In the final section of this chapter, I have speculated about the influence of developers' psychological type preferences on their practice. Although we may want to view developers as "above all of that" and capable of superhuman feats of meeting all needs at all times, they are in fact people with preferences just as are educators and learners. We in adult education must bring together the various threads of what we do: the characteristics of educators, learners, and developers; the reality of working within a teaching context within an organization or community; and the influence of cultural values and expectations. Diversity brings power to our practice, but only when we understand our diversity.

References

Adams, F. "Highlander Folk School: Getting Information, Going Back and Teaching It." *Harvard Educational Review,* 1972, *42*(4), 497–520.

Addleton, R. L., Jr. "Self-Directed Learning Projects of Continuing Educators in Selected Alabama Four Year Colleges and Universities." Unpublished doctoral dissertation, University of Alabama, 1984. *Dissertation Abstracts International, 44*(10A), 2988.

Amundsen, C., Gryspeerdt, D., and Moxness, K. "Practice-Centred Inquiry: Developing More Effective Teaching." *Review of Higher Education,* 1993, *16*(3), 329–353.

Angelo, T. A., and Cross, P. *Classroom Assessment Techniques: A Handbook for Faculty.* Ann Arbor: The University of Michigan, 1988.

Apps, J. W. *Leadership for the Emerging Age: Transforming Practice in Adult and Continuing Education.* San Francisco: Jossey-Bass, 1994.

Argyris, C. *Management and Organizational Development.* New York: McGraw-Hill, 1971.

Austin, A. E. "Supporting the Professor as Teacher: The Lilly Teaching Fellows Program." *The Review of Higher Education,* 1992, *16*(1), 85–106.

Bagnall, R. G. "Discriminative Justice and Responsibility in Postmodernist Adult Education." *Adult Education Quarterly,* 1995, *45*(2), 79–94.

Bandura, A. *Social Learning Theory.* Englewood Cliffs, N.J.: Prentice-Hall, 1977.

Banta, T. W., and Associates. *Making a Difference: Outcomes of a Decade of Assessment in Higher Education.* San Francisco: Jossey-Bass, 1993.

Bard, R., Bell, C. R., Stephen, L., and Webster, L. *The Trainer's Professional Development Handbook.* San Francisco: Jossey-Bass, 1987.

Baskett, H.K.M. "Processes Involved with Developing Autonomous Learning Competencies." In H. B. Long and Associates (eds.), *SDL: Consensus and Conflict.* Norman: Oklahoma Research Center for Continuing Professional and Higher Education, University of Oklahoma, 1991.

Baskett, H.K.M. "The 'Nanosecond Nineties': Challenges and Opportunities in Continuing Professional Education." *Adult Learning,* 1993, *4*(6), 15–17.

Belenky, M. F., Clinchy, B. M., Goldberger, N. G., and Tarule, J. M. *Women's Ways of Knowing.* New York: Basic Books, 1986.

Best, J. W., and Kahn, J. V. *Research in Education.* (5th ed.) Englewood Cliffs, N.J.: Prentice-Hall, 1986.

Borgstrom, L., and Olofsson, L. "Participation in Study Circles and the Creation of Individual Resources." *Proceedings of the Adult Education Research Conference,* no. 24. Montreal: Concordia University, University of Montreal, 1983.

Boshier, R. "Educational Participation and Dropout: A Theoretical Model." *Adult Education,* 1973, *23,* 255–282.

Boshier, R. "A Conceptual Framework for Analyzing the Training of Trainers and Adult Educators." In S. Brookfield (ed.), *Training Educators of Adults.* London: Routledge, 1988.

Boshier, R. "A Topography of Adult Education Theory and Research." *Proceedings of the Adult Education Research Conference,* no. 35. Knoxville: University of Tennessee, May 1994.

Boud, D., Keough, R., and Walker, D. (eds.). *Reflection: Turning Experience into Learning.* London: Kogan Page, 1985.

Boud, D., and Walker, D. *Experience and Learning: Reflection at Work.* Geelong, Australia: Deakin University Press, 1991.

Boud, D., and Walker, D. "In the Midst of Experience: Developing a Model to Aid Learners and Facilitators." In R. Harris and P. Willis (eds.), *Striking a Balance: Adult and Community Education in Australia Towards 2000.* University of South Australia: Centre for Human Resource Studies, 1992.

Boyd, R. D., and Myers, J. G. "Transformative Education." *International Journal of Lifelong Education,* 1988, *7*(4), 261–284.

Boyle, G. *Father Tompkins of Nova Scotia.* New York: Kennedy and Sons, 1953.

Brandt, D., and Sell, R. "The Development of Problem Solving Skills in Engineering Students in Context." *European Journal of Engineering Education,* 1986, *11*(1), 59–65.

Brockett, R. G. "Professional Development, Artistry, and Style." In R. G. Brockett (ed.), *Professional Development for Educators of Adults.* New Directions for Adult and Continuing Education, no. 51. San Francisco: Jossey-Bass, 1991a.

Brockett, R. G. (ed.). *Professional Development for Educators of Adults.* New Directions for Adult and Continuing Education, no. 51. San Francisco: Jossey-Bass, 1991b.

Brookfield, S. *Understanding and Facilitating Adult Learning.* San Francisco: Jossey-Bass, 1986.

Brookfield, S. *Developing Critical Thinkers: Challenging Adults to Explore Alternative Ways of Thinking and Acting*. San Francisco: Jossey-Bass, 1987.

Brookfield, S. *The Skillful Teacher*. San Francisco: Jossey-Bass, 1990a.

Brookfield, S. "The Influence of Media on Learners' Perspectives." In J. Mezirow and Associates (eds.), *Fostering Critical Reflection in Adulthood: A Guide to Transformative and Emancipatory Learning*. San Francisco: Jossey-Bass, 1990b.

Brookfield, S. "Self-Directed Learning, Political Clarity, and the Critical Practice of Adult Education." *Adult Education Quarterly*, 1993, *43*(4), 227–242.

Brookfield, S. "Tales from the Dark Side: A Phenomenography of Adult Critical Reflection." *Proceedings of the Adult Education Research Conference*, no. 35. Knoxville: The University of Tennessee, May 1994.

Butler Research Associates. *Exploratory Research on Trainer Skills in Ontario*. Internal Report. Toronto: Ontario Training Corporation, 1989.

Campbell, V. N. "Self-Direction and Programmed Instruction for Five Different Types of Learning Objectives." *Psychology in the Schools*, 1964, *1*(4), 348–359.

Candy, P. C. *Self-Direction for Lifelong Learning*. San Francisco: Jossey-Bass, 1991.

CareerTrack. *Excellence as a First-Time Supervisor*. Boulder, Colo.: Career-Track, 1995.

Carr, W., and Kemmis, S. *Becoming Critical: Education, Knowledge and Action Research*. Philadelphia: Falmer Press, 1986.

Castner, B., and Jordan, W. "Professional Trainers Go to School." *Training and Development Journal*, July 1989, pp. 77–79.

Cavanaugh, S. H. "Continuing Education and Practice." In L. Curry, J. F. Wergin, and Associates (eds.), *Educating Professionals: Responding to New Expectations for Competence and Accountability*. San Francisco: Jossey-Bass, 1993.

Centra, J. *Reflective Faculty Evaluation: Enhancing Teaching and Determining Faculty Effectiveness*. San Francisco: Jossey-Bass, 1993.

Cervero, R. M. "Professional Practice, Learning, and Continuing Education: An Integrated Perspective." *Professions Educator Research Notes*, 1989, *11*, 10–13.

Clark, M. C. "Transformational Learning." In S. B. Merriam (ed.), *An Update on Adult Learning Theory*. New Directions for Adult and Continuing Education, no. 57. San Francisco: Jossey-Bass, 1993.

Clark, M. C., Caffarella, R. S., and Ingram, P. B. "The View From Beneath the Ceiling: The Link Between Development and Practice for Women in Midmanagement Leadership Roles." *Proceedings of the Adult Education Research Conference,* no. 35. Knoxville: The University of Tennessee, May 1994.

Clark, M. C., and Wilson, A. L. "Context and Rationality in Mezirow's Theory of Transformational Learning." *Adult Education Quarterly,* 1991, *41*(2), 75–91.

Collard, S., and Law, M. "The Limits of Perspective Transformation: A Critique of Mezirow's Theory." *Adult Education Quarterly,* 1989, *39,* 99–107.

Collins, M. "Self-Directed Learning or an Emancipatory Practice of Adult Education: Re-Thinking the Role of the Adult Educator." *Proceedings of the Adult Education Research Conference,* no. 29. Calgary: University of Calgary, May 1988.

Collins, M. "From Self-Directed Learning to Postmodernist Thought in Adult Education: Relocating our Object of Theory and Practice." *Proceedings of the Adult Education Research Conference,* no. 35. Knoxville: University of Tennessee, May 1994.

Conti, G. J. "Assessing Teaching Style in Adult Education: How and Why?" *Lifelong Learning,* 1985, *6*(88), 7–11, 28.

Courtney, S., and Dirkx, J. "Editorial." *Adult Education Quarterly,* 1994, *44,* 63.

Cranton, P. "The Interaction Between Learner Characteristics and Degree of Learner Control in CAI." Unpublished doctoral dissertation, University of Toronto, 1976.

Cranton, P. *Working with Adult Learners.* Toronto: Wall & Emerson, 1992.

Cranton, P. "Reflective Teaching Evaluation." *Ideas.* St. Catharines, Ontario: Brock University Instructional Development Office, 1993.

Cranton, P. *Understanding and Promoting Transformative Learning: A Guide for Educators of Adults.* San Francisco: Jossey-Bass, 1994a.

Cranton, P. "Self-Directed and Transformative Instructional Development." *Journal of Higher Education,* 1994b, *65*(6), 726–744.

Cranton, P., and Knoop, R. "Incorporating Job Satisfaction into a Model of Instructional Effectiveness." In M. Theall and J. Franklin (eds.), *Effective Practices for Improving Teaching.* New Directions for Teaching and Learning, no. 48. San Francisco: Jossey-Bass, 1991.

Cranton, P., and Knoop, R. *Self-Subordinate Review Process: Final Report.* Ottawa, Ontario: Department of Indian and Northern Affairs, 1993.

Cranton, P., and Knoop, R. "Assessing Psychological Type: The PET Type Check." *General, Social, and Genetic Psychological Monographs,* 1995a, *121*(2), pp. 247–274.

Cranton, P., and Knoop, R. "Psychological Types and Learning Styles." St. Catharines, Ontario: PET Professional Effectiveness Technologies, 1995b.

Cranton, P., and Knoop, R. "Psychological Types and Teaching Styles," St. Catharines, Ontario: PET Professional Effectiveness Technologies, 1995c.

Cross, P. "Classroom Research: Helping Professors Learn More About Teaching and Learning." In P. Seldin (ed.), *How Administrators Can Improve Teaching*. San Francisco: Jossey-Bass, 1990.

Cross, P. *Adults as Learners*. San Francisco: Jossey-Bass, 1992.

Crowe-Joong, E. "Evidence of the Effectiveness of a Problem-Based Learning Approach in the Medical Curriculum." In P. Stortz (ed.), *Higher Education Group Annual 1992/93*. Toronto: Ontario Institute for Studies in Education, 1993.

Cummings, T. G., and Huse, E. F. *Organization Development and Change*. (4th ed.) St. Paul, Minn.: West, 1989.

Curry, L., Wergin, J. F., and Associates (eds.). *Educating Professions: Responding to New Expectations for Competence and Accountability*. San Francisco: Jossey-Bass, 1993.

Daloz, L. *Effective Teaching and Mentoring: Realizing the Transformational Power of Adult Learning Experiences*. San Francisco: Jossey-Bass, 1986.

Danis, C., and Tremblay, N. A. "Critical Analysis of Adult Learning Principles from a Self-Directed Learner's Perspective." *Proceedings of the Adult Education Research Conference*, no. 26. Arizona State University, Temple, May 1985.

Danis, C., and Tremblay, N. A. "Propositions Regarding Autodidactic Learning and Their Implications for Teaching." *Lifelong Learning: An Omnibus of Practice and Research*, 1987, *10*(7), 4–7.

Davis, L. N. *Planning, Conducting, and Evaluating Workshops*. Austin, Tex.: Learning Concepts, 1974.

De Bono, E. *The Use of Lateral Thinking*. Harmondsworth, England: Penguin Books, 1971.

Dearden, R. F. "Autonomy and Education." In R. F. Dearden, P. H. Hirst, and R. S. Peters (eds.), *Education and the Development of Reason*. London: Routledge & Kegan Paul, 1972.

Delahaye, B. L., Limerick, D. C., and Hearn, G. "The Relationship Between Andragogical and Pedagogical Orientations and the Implications for Adult Learning." *Adult Education Quarterly*, 1994, *44*(4), 187–200.

Dewey, J. *How We Think*. Chicago: Regnery, 1933.

Dirkx, J. M. "Self-Reflection in Clinical Education: Using Group Process to Improve Practitioner-Client Relationships." Paper presented at the annual meeting of the American Educational Research Association, San Francisco, March 1989.

Dirkx, J. M., Lavin, R., Spurgin, M., and Holder, B. "Continuing Education as a Practical Problem: A Model for Vocational Educators?" *Journal of Vocational and Technical Education,* 1993, *9*(2), 41–54.

Dirkx, J. M., and others. "Conceptions of Transformation in Adult Education: Views of Self, Society, and Social Change." In D. Flannery (ed.), *Proceedings of the Adult Education Research Conference,* no. 34. University Park: Pennsylvania State University, May 1993.

Dolmans, D. J. M., Gijselaers, W. H., Schmidt, H. G., and Van Der Meer, S. B. "Problem Effectiveness in a Course Using Problem-Based Learning." *Academic Medicine,* 1993, *68*(3), 207–213.

Dubin, R., and Taveggia, T. C. *The Teaching-Learning Paradox: A Comparative Analysis of College Teaching Methods.* Eugene: Center for the Advanced Study of Educational Administration, University of Oregon, 1968.

Eble, K. E. *The Craft of Teaching: A Guide to Mastering the Professor's Art.* (2nd ed.) San Francisco: Jossey-Bass, 1988.

Elden, M., and Gjersvik, R. "Democratizing Action Research at Work: A Scandinavian Model." In A. Brooks and K. E. Watkins (eds.), *The Emerging Power of Action Inquiry Technologies.* New Directions for Adult and Continuing Education, no. 63. San Francisco: Jossey-Bass, 1994.

Ellsworth, J. H. "Dr. E's Eclectic Compendium of Electronic Resources for Adult/Distance Education." je01@academia.swt.edu. (Available via FTP at host: una.hh.lib.umich.edu, path: /inetdirsstacks, file: disted.ellsworth), 1993.

Erikson, E. H. "Identity and the Life Cycle." *Psychological Issues,* 1959, *1,* Monograph No. 1.

Ewert, G. "Habermas and Education: A Comprehensive Overview of the Influence of Habermas in Educational Literature." *Review of Educational Research,* 1991, *61,* 345–378.

Eyerman, R., and Jamison, A. *Social Movements: A Cognitive Approach.* Cambridge: Polity Press, 1991.

Field, L. D. "An Investigation into the Structure, Validity, and Reliability of Guglielmino's Self-Directed Learning Readiness Scale." *Adult Education Quarterly,* 1989, *39*(3), 125–139.

Flew, A. *A Dictionary of Philosophy.* (2nd ed.) New York: St. Martin's Press, 1984.

Foucault, M. *The Archaeology of Knowledge and the Discourse on Language.* (A. M. Sheridan Smith, trans.). New York: Pantheon, 1972.

Freire, P. *Pedagogy of the Oppressed.* New York: Herder and Herder, 1970.

Fromm, E. *Fear of Freedom*. London: Routledge, 1946.

Gage, N. *Teacher Education and Teacher Effectiveness*. Palo Alto, Calif.: Pacific Books, 1977.

Gass, M., Goldman, K., and Priest, S. "Constructing Effective Adventure Training Programs." *Journal of Experiential Education*, 1992, *15*(1), 35–42.

Gay, G. "Interaction of Learner-Control and Prior Understanding in Computer-Assisted Video Instruction." *Journal of Educational Psychology*, 1986, *78*(3), 225–227.

Geis, G. L. *As Training Moves Toward the Next Decade: A Needs Analysis of Professional Development for Trainers*. Toronto: Ontario Training Corporation, 1991.

Giroux, H. A. "Modernism, Postmodernism, and Feminism: Rethinking the Boundaries of Educational Discourse." In H. A. Giroux (ed.), *Postmodernism, Feminism, and Cultural Politics*. Albany: State University of New York Press, 1991.

Glazer, N. "Schools of the Minor Professions." *Minerva*, 1974, *12* (3), 346–363.

Gould, R. L. "Adulthood." In H. Kaplan and B. Sadock (eds.), *Comprehensive Textbook of Psychiatry*. (5th ed.) Baltimore: Williams & Wilkins, 1989.

Gould, R. L. "The Therapeutic Learning Program." In J. Mezirow and Associates (eds.), *Fostering Critical Reflection in Adulthood: A Guide to Transformative and Emancipatory Learning*. San Francisco: Jossey-Bass, 1990.

Griffin, C. *Adult Education and Social Policy*. London: Croom Helm, 1987.

Griffin, C. "A Critical Perspective on Sociology and Adult Education." In J. M. Peters, P. Jarvis, and Associates (eds.), *Adult Education: Evolution and Achievements in a Developing Field of Study*. San Francisco: Jossey-Bass, 1991.

Group for Collaborative Inquiry. "The Democratization of Knowledge." *Adult Education Quarterly*, 1993, *44*(1), 43–51.

Guglielmino, L. M. "Development of the Self-Directed Learning Readiness Scale." Unpublished doctoral dissertation, University of Georgia, 1977. *Dissertation Abstracts International, 38*(11A), 6467.

Habermas, J. *Knowledge and Human Interests*. Boston: Beacon Press, 1971.

Habermas, J. *Legitimation Crisis*. London: Heinemann, 1976.

Habermas, J. "Modernity: An Incomplete Project." In H. Foster (ed.), *The Anti-Aesthetic: Essays on Postmodern Culture*. Seattle: Bay Press, 1983.

Habermas, J. *The Theory of Communicative Action*. Boston: Beacon Press, 1984.

Habermas, J. "Hermeneutics and the Social Sciences." In K. Mueller-Vollmer, (ed.), *The Hermeneutics Reader.* New York: Continuum, 1989.

Hargreaves, A., and Fullan, M. G. (eds.). *Understanding Teacher Development.* New York: Teachers College Press, 1992.

Harris, I. B. "New Expectations for Professional Competence." In L. Curry, J. F. Wergin, and Associates (eds.), *Educating Professionals: Responding to New Expectations for Competence and Accountability.* San Francisco: Jossey-Bass, 1993.

Hart, M. "Liberation Through Consciousness Raising." In J. Mezirow and Associates (eds.), *Fostering Critical Reflection in Adulthood: A Guide to Transformative and Emancipatory Learning.* San Francisco: Jossey-Bass, 1990.

Heimlich, J. E., and Norland, E. *Developing Teaching Style in Adult Education.* San Francisco: Jossey-Bass, 1994.

Held, D. *Introduction to Critical Theory: Horkheimer to Habermas,* Berkeley: University of California Press, 1980.

Henry, G. T., and Basile, K. C. "Understanding the Decision to Participate in Formal Adult Education." *Adult Education Quarterly,* 1994, *44*(2), 64–82.

Herbeson, E. "Personality Type and Self-Directed Learning." *The Canadian School Executive,* 1992, *12,* 8–15.

Hersey, P., and Blanchard, K. H. *Management of Organizational Behavior: Utilizing Human Resources.* (4th ed.) Englewood Cliffs, N.J.: Prentice-Hall, 1982.

Holford, J. "Why Social Movements Matter: Adult Education Theory, Cognitive Praxis, and the Creation of Knowledge." *Adult Education Quarterly,* 1995, *45*(2), 95–111.

Holland, R. "George Kelly: Constructive, Innocent and Reluctant Existentialist." In D. Bannister (ed.), *Perspectives in Personal Construct Theory.* London: Academic Press, 1970.

Houle, C. O. *Continuing Learning in the Professions.* San Francisco: Jossey-Bass, 1980.

Imel, S. "Information Resources for Professional Development." In R. G. Brockett (ed.), *Professional Development for Educators of Adults.* New Directions for Adult and Continuing Education, no. 51. San Francisco: Jossey-Bass, 1991.

Jarvis, P. "Learning Practical Knowledge." In H.K.M. Baskett and V. J. Marsick (eds.), *Professionals' Ways of Knowing: New Findings on How to Improve Professional Education.* New Directions in Adult and Continuing Education, no. 55. San Francisco: Jossey-Bass, 1992a.

Jarvis, P. *Paradoxes of Learning: On Becoming an Individual in Society.* San Francisco: Jossey-Bass, 1992b.

Jung, C. *Psychological Types*. Princeton, N.J.: Princeton University Press, 1971. (Originally published 1921.)

Keenan, W. J. "Are You Overspending on Training?" *Sales and Marketing Management*, 1990, *142*(1), 56–60.

Kellner, D. "Reading Images Critically: Toward a Postmodern Pedagogy." In H. A. Giroux (ed.), *Postmodernism, Feminism, and Cultural Politics*. Albany: State University of New York Press, 1991.

Kelly, G. A. *The Psychology of Personal Constructs*. Vols. 1 and 2. New York: Norton, 1955.

Kelly, G. A. *A Theory of Personality*. Norton: New York, 1963.

Kincheloe, J. L. *Teachers as Researchers: Qualitative Inquiry as a Path to Empowerment*. London: Falmer Press, 1991.

King, P. M., and Kitchener, K. S. *Developing Reflective Judgment*. San Francisco: Jossey-Bass, 1994.

Knoop, R. *Charismatic and Transformative Leadership Tendencies and Psychological Types*. St. Catharines, Ontario: PET Professional Effectiveness Technologies, 1995.

Knowles, M. S. *Self-Directed Learning*. Chicago: Follett, 1975.

Knowles, M. S. *The Modern Practice of Adult Education*. (2nd ed.) Chicago: Association Press, 1980.

Knox, A. *Adult Development and Learning*. San Francisco: Jossey-Bass, 1977.

Knox, A. "Comparative Perspectives on Professionals' Ways of Knowing," In H.K.M. Baskett and V. J. Marsick (eds.), *Professionals' Ways of Knowing: New Findings on How to Improve Professional Education*, New Directions for Adult and Continuing Education, no. 55. San Francisco: Jossey-Bass, 1992.

Knox, A. *Strengthening Adult and Continuing Education: A Global Perspective on Synergistic Leadership*. San Francisco: Jossey-Bass, 1993.

Kolb, D. A. *Experiential Learning: Experience as a Source of Learning and Development*. Englewood Cliffs, N.J.: Prentice-Hall, 1984.

Kreber, C. "The Influence of Faculty's Teaching Philosophy and Behavior on Students' Critical Thinking and Self-Directedness." Paper presented at the Society for Teaching and Learning in Higher Education, Calgary, Alberta, June, 1994.

Kreber, C. *Action Research in Higher Education*. St. Catharines, Ontario: Brock University Instructional Development Office, 1995.

Krishnamurti, J. *Think on These Things*. New York: Harper & Row, 1964.

Levinson-Rose, J., and Menges, R. "Improving College Teaching: A Critical Review of Research." *Review of Educational Research*, 1981, *51*(3), 265–273.

Lewin, K. "Action Research and Minority Problems." *Journal of Social Issues*, 1946, *2*, 34–36.

Lewin, K. "Frontiers in Group Dynamics: Concept, Method, and Reality in Social Science." *Human Relations,* 1947, *1,* 5–41.

Lewin, K. "Resolving Social Conflicts." In G. Weiss Lewin (ed.), *Selected Papers on Group Dynamics.* New York: Harper and Brothers, 1948.

Lindeman, E. C. *The Meaning of Adult Education.* New York: New Republic, 1926.

Long, H. B. "Item Analysis of Guglielmino's Self-Directed Learning Readiness Scale." *International Journal of Lifelong Education,* 1987, *6*(4), 331–336.

Long, H. B. "Challenging Some Myths about Self-Directed Learning Research." In H. B. Long and Associates (eds.), *New Ideas About Self-Directed Learning.* Norman: Oklahoma Research Center for Continuing Professional and Higher Education of the University of Oklahoma, 1994.

Long, H. B., and Associates (eds.). *New Ideas About Self-Directed Learning.* Norman: Oklahoma Research Center for Continuing Professional and Higher Education of the University of Oklahoma, 1994.

McLagan, P. A. "Who Can Plan? You Can!" *Training and Development Journal,* 1987, *41*(7), 27–33.

McLagan, P. A. *Models for HRD Practice: The Models.* Arlington, Va.: American Society for Training and Development, 1989.

McLaren, P. "Schooling the Postmodern Body: Critical Pedagogy and the Politics of Enfleshment." In H. Giroux (ed.), *Postmodernism, Feminism, and Cultural Politics.* New York: State University of New York Press, 1991.

Macquarrie, J. *Existentialism.* Harmondsworth, England: Pelican, 1973.

Mager, R. F. *Preparing Instructional Objectives.* San Francisco: Fearon, 1962.

Maher, F. A. "Toward a Richer Theory of Feminist Pedagogy: A Comparison of 'Liberation' and 'Gender' Models for Teaching and Learning." *Journal of Education,* 1987, *169*(3), 91–100.

Marsh, H. W. "Students' Evaluation of University Teaching: Research Findings, Methodological Issues, and Directions for Future Research." *International Journal of Educational Research,* 1987, *11,* 253–388.

Marsick, V. J., and Watkins, K. *Informal and Incidental Learning in the Workplace.* London: Routledge, 1990.

Maslow, A. H. *Motivation and Personality.* New York: Harper & Row, 1954.

Maslow, A. H. *Motivation and Personality.* (2nd ed.) New York: Harper & Row, 1970.

Merriam, S. B. (ed.). *An Update on Adult Learning Theory.* New Directions for Adult and Continuing Education, no. 57. San Francisco: Jossey-Bass, 1993.

Merriam, S. B., and Caffarella, R. S. *Learning in Adulthood*. San Francisco: Jossey-Bass, 1991.

Meyers, C. *Teaching Students to Think Critically: A Guide for Faculty in all Disciplines*. San Francisco: Jossey-Bass, 1986.

Mezirow, J. "A Critical Theory of Self-Directed Learning." In S. Brookfield (ed.), *Self-Directed Learning: From Theory to Practice*. New Directions for Adult and Continuing Education, no. 25. San Francisco: Jossey-Bass, 1985.

Mezirow, J. "Principles of Good Practice in Continuing Education." In S. Brookfield (ed.), *Training Educators of Adults*. London: Routledge, 1988.

Mezirow, J. "Conclusion: Toward Transformative Learning and Emancipatory Education." In J. Mezirow and Associates (eds.), *Fostering Critical Reflection in Adulthood: A Guide to Transformative and Emancipatory Education*. San Francisco: Jossey-Bass, 1990.

Mezirow, J. "Transformation Theory and Social Action: A Response to Collard and Law." *Adult Education Quarterly*, 1989, *39*, 169–175.

Mezirow, J. *Transformative Dimensions of Adult Learning*. San Francisco: Jossey-Bass, 1991.

Mezirow, J. "Understanding Transformation Theory." *Adult Education Quarterly*, 1994, *44*(4), 222–232.

Mezirow, J., and Associates (eds.). *Fostering Critical Reflection in Adulthood: A Guide to Transformative and Emancipatory Education*. San Francisco: Jossey-Bass, 1990.

Millar, C. J., Morphet, A. R., and Saddington, J. A. "Case Study: Curriculum Negotiation in Professional Adult Education." *Journal of Curriculum Studies*, 1986, *18*(4), 429–442.

Miller, H. L. *Participation of Adults in Education: A Force-Field Analysis*. Boston: Center for the Study of Liberal Education for Adults, Boston University, 1967.

Moore, W. *The Professions*. New York: Russell Sage Foundation, 1970.

Mott, V. W. "The Role of Intuition in the Reflective Practice of Adult Education." *Proceedings of the Adult Education Research Conference*, no. 35. Knoxville: The University of Tennessee, May 1994.

Mueller-Vollmer, K. (ed.). *The Hermeneutics Reader*. New York: Continuum, 1989.

Myers, I. B. *Gifts Differing*. (7th ed.) Palo Alto, Calif.: Consulting Psychologists Press, 1985.

Newman, M. "Response to Understanding Transformation Theory." *Adult Education Quarterly*, 1994, *44*(4), 236–242.

Niagara Institute. *Working with Others*. Niagara-on-the-Lake, Ontario: Niagara Institute, 1994.

Oddi, L. F. "Development of an Instrument to Measure Self-Directed Continuous Learning." Unpublished doctoral dissertation, Northern Illinois University, 1984. *Dissertation Abstracts International, 46*(01A), 49.

Perry, W. J., Jr. *Forms of Intellectual and Ethical Development in the College Years: A Scheme.* Troy, Mo.: Holt, Rinehart & Winston, 1970.

Peters, J. M. "Strategies for Reflective Practice." In R. G. Brockett (ed.), *Professional Development for Educators of Adults.* New Directions for Adult and Continuing Education, no. 51. San Francisco: Jossey-Bass, 1991.

Peters, J. M. "Instructors-As-Researchers-and-Theorists: Action Research in a Community College." *Proceedings of the Adult Education Research Conference,* no. 35. Knoxville: The University of Tennessee, May 1994.

Pierce, J., Glass, G., Young, M., and Soucy, D. "The Educational Research List (ERL-L) on Bitnet/Internet." *Educational Researcher,* 1994, *23*(2), 25–28.

Piskurich, G. M. *Self-Directed Learning: A Practical Guide to Design, Development, and Implementation.* San Francisco: Jossey-Bass, 1993.

Quinlan, K. M. "About Teaching and Learning Centers." *AAHE Bulletin,* 1991, *44,* 11–16.

Renner, P. F. *The Instructor's Survival Kit.* (2nd ed.) Vancouver: Training Associates, 1983.

Rice, R. E., and Richlin, L. "Broadening the Concept of Scholarship in the Professions." In L. Curry, J. F. Wergin, and Associates (eds.), *Educating Professionals: Responding to New Expectations for Competence and Accountability.* San Francisco: Jossey-Bass, 1993.

Robbins, S. P., and Stuart-Kotze, R. *Management.* (4th ed.) Englewood Cliffs, N.J.: Prentice-Hall, 1994.

Rogers, C. R. *Freedom to Learn: A View of What Education Might Become.* Columbus, Ohio: Merrill, 1969.

Rosenberg, M. J. "Performance Technology: Working the System." *Training,* 1990, *27*(2), 43–48.

Rosenblum, S., and Darkenwald, G. G. "Effects of Adult Learner Participation in Course Planning on Achievement and Satisfaction." *Adult Education Quarterly,* 1983, *33*(3), 147–153.

Roth, I. "Challenging Habits of Expectation." In J. Mezirow and Associates (eds.), *Fostering Critical Reflection in Adulthood: A Guide to Transformative and Emancipatory Learning.* San Francisco: Jossey-Bass, 1990.

Russell, T., and Munby, H. (eds.). *Teachers and Teaching.* London: Falmer Press, 1992.

Schlattner, C. J. "The Body in Transformative Learning." *Proceedings of the Adult Education Research Conference,* no. 35. Knoxville: The University of Tennessee, 1994.

Schön, D. A. *The Reflective Practitioner.* New York: Basic Books, 1983.

Schön, D. A. *Educating the Reflective Practitioner.* San Francisco: Jossey-Bass, 1987.

Schön, D. A. (ed.). *The Reflective Turn.* New York: Teachers College Press, 1991.

Selman, G. "The Enemies of Adult Education." *Canadian Journal of University Continuing Education,* 1989, *15,* 68–81.

Selman, G., and Dampier, P. *The Foundations of Adult Education in Canada.* Toronto, Ontario: Thompson Educational Publishing, 1991.

Sharp, D. *Personality Types: Jung's Model of Typology.* Toronto, Ontario: Inner City Books, 1987.

Shelton, E., and Spikes, W. F. "Leadership Through Professional Associations." In R. G. Brockett (ed.), *Professional Development for Educators of Adults.* New Directions for Adult and Continuing Education, no. 51. San Francisco: Jossey-Bass, 1991.

Smith, R., and Schwartz, F. "A Theory of Effectiveness: Faculty Development Case Studies." In J. R. Jeffrey and G. R. Erickson (eds.), *To Improve the Academy.* Vol. 4. Stillwater, Okla.: Professional and Organizational Network in Higher Education and New Forums Press, 1985, 63–74.

Sork, T. (ed.). *Designing and Implementing Effective Workshops.* New Directions for Adult and Continuing Education, no. 22. San Francisco: Jossey-Bass, 1984.

Spikes, W. F. "Developing Our Own Professional Associations and Building Bridges to Others." In B. A. Quigley (ed.), *Fulfilling the Promise of Adult and Continuing Education.* New Directions for Continuing Education, no. 44. San Francisco: Jossey-Bass, 1989.

Stalker, J. "Voluntary Participation: Deconstructing the Myth." *Adult Education Quarterly,* 1993, *43*(2), 63–75.

Stubblefield, H. W. "Making the Most of Professional Reading." In R. G. Brockett (ed.), *Professional Development for Educators of Adults.* New Directions for Adult and Continuing Education, no. 51. San Francisco: Jossey-Bass, 1991.

Tennant, M. C. "Perspective Transformative and Adult Development." *Adult Education Quarterly,* 1993, *44*(1), 34–42.

Tennant, M. C., and Pogson, P. *Learning and Change in the Adult Years: A Developmental Perspective.* San Francisco: Jossey-Bass, 1995.

Theall, M., and Franklin, J. (eds.). *Effective Practices for Improving Teaching.* New Directions for Teaching and Learning, no. 48. San Francisco: Jossey-Bass, 1991.

thINQ. "Phenomenology as an Interpretive Frame: The Evolution of a

Research Method for Understanding How Learning Is Experienced in Collaborative Inquiry Groups." *Proceedings of the Adult Education Research Conference,* no. 35. Knoxville: The University of Tennessee, May 1994.

Tisdell, E. J. "Feminism and Adult Learning: Power, Pedagogy, and Praxis." In S. B. Merriam (ed.), *An Update on Adult Learning Theory.* New Directions for Adult and Continuing Education, no. 57, San Francisco: Jossey-Bass, 1993.

Tough, A. M. *The Adult's Learning Projects: A Fresh Approach to Theory and Practice in Adult Learning.* (Rev. ed.) Toronto: Ontario Institute for Studies in Education, 1979.

Tremblay, N. "L'aide à l'apprentissage en situation d'autodidaxie" [Help with learning in autodidactic situations]. Unpublished doctoral dissertation, University of Montreal, 1981.

Tremmel, R. "Zen and the Art of Reflective Practice in Teacher Education." *Harvard Educational Review,* 1993, *63*(4), 434–458.

Wang, M. C. "Development and Consequences of Students' Sense of Personal Control." In J. M. Levine and M. C. Wang (eds.), *Teacher and Student Perceptions: Implications for Learning.* Hillsdale, N.J.: Erlbaum, 1983.

Watkins, K. E., and Marsick, V. J. *Sculpting the Learning Organization: Lessons in the Art and Science of Systemic Change.* San Francisco: Jossey-Bass, 1993.

Watson, G., and Glaser, E. M. *Critical Thinking Appraisal Manual.* Orlando, Fla.: Harcourt Brace Jovanovich, 1980.

Weathersby, R. "Ego Development." In A. W. Chickering (ed.), *The Modern American College.* San Francisco: Jossey-Bass, 1981.

Wellins, R. S., Byham, W. C., and Wilson, J. M. *Empowered Teams: Creating Self-Directed Work Groups That Improve Quality, Productivity, and Participation.* San Francisco: Jossey-Bass, 1991.

Wells, D. *Empty Promises: Quality of Working Life Programs and the Labor Movement.* New York: Monthly Review Press, 1987.

Welton, M. R. "The Contribution of Critical Theory to Our Understanding of Adult Learning." In S. B. Merriam (ed.), *An Update on Adult Learning Theory.* New Directions for Adult and Continuing Education, no. 57. San Francisco: Jossey-Bass, 1993.

West, R., and Bentley, E. "Structural Analysis of the Self-Directed Learning Readiness Scale: A Confirmatory Factor Analysis Using LISREL Modeling." Paper presented at the 3rd North American Symposium on Adult Self-Directed Learning, University of Oklahoma, Feb. 1989.

Wilcox, S. *Instructor Support for Self-Directed Learning in Higher Education.*

Unpublished master's thesis. St. Catharines, Ontario: Brock University, 1990.

Wilson, A. L. "The Common Concern: Controlling the Professionalization of Adult Education." *Adult Education Quarterly*, 1993, *44*, 1–16.

Wilson, D. N. *An International Perspective on Trainer Competencies, Standards and Certification.* Toronto: Ontario Training Corporation, 1992.

Wlodkowski, R. J. *Enhancing Adult Motivation to Learn.* San Francisco: Jossey-Bass, 1990.

Zeph, C. P. "Graduate Study as Professional Development." In R. G. Brockett (ed.), *Professional Development for Educators of Adults.* New Directions for Adult and Continuing Education, no. 51. San Francisco: Jossey-Bass, 1991.

Zuber-Skerritt, O. *Professional Development in Higher Education: A Theoretical Framework for Action Research.* London: Kogan Page, 1992.

Index

A

Abuse, 108

Action research, 21; applied to educator development, 163, 188–191, 201; applied to social reform, 144–146, 159–160; and psychological type, 199–200

Adams, F., 15

Addleton, R. L., Jr., 70

Adult education. *See* Practice

Adult Education Association, 149

Adult Education Quarterly, 18, 169–170

Adult educators: as agents of change, 140–161; attitudes of, towards social reform, 152–153, 162–163; in business and industry, 9–11; in colleges, 8–9; in community education, 13–14; within the community of educators, 149–152; in context of setting, 6–16, 21–24; diversity of, 5–6, 162; in health professions, 11–13, 158–160; individual differences among, 118–139, 155–156; in informal settings, 14–16; knowledge types and, 21–24; meaning perspectives of, 96–103; meaning perspectives distortions of, 103–109; in organizational work set-

tings, 143–148, 158–160; professional developers for, 182–202; socialization of, 141–142, 148; within society, 152–155; in universities, 7–8. *See also* Business/industry educators; College educators; Developers for adult educators; Development, educator; Health profession educators; University educators

Alternatives, imagining of, 90–93; individual differences and, 92, 131

American Association for Adult and Continuing Education, 5, 149

American Association of Adult Education, 149

American Society for Training and Development, 10

Amundsen, G., 8, 34, 192

Andragogy, 111

Angelo, T. A., 189–190

Antigonish Movement, 15

Apprenticeship, 27

Apps, J. W., 22–23

Argyris, C., 144, 160

Art, 91

Assessment, of personal characteristics, 120–122. *See also* Psychological types; Quantitative empirical methodology

Assumptions, 5; articulating of,

219